THE ROMAN ARMY
LEGIONS, WARS AND CAMPAIGNS

THE ROMAN ARMY

LEGIONS, WARS AND CAMPAIGNS

a military history of the world's first superpower from the rise of
the republic and the might of the empire to the fall of the west

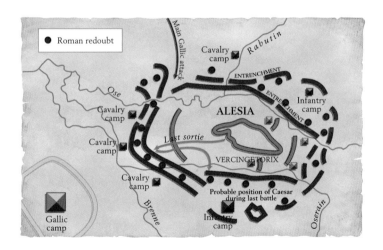

NIGEL RODGERS
consultant:
DR. HAZEL DODGE FSA

southwater

For my father

This edition is published by Southwater
an imprint of Anness Publishing Ltd
Hermes House, 88–89 Blackfriars Road, London SE1 8HA
tel. 020 7401 2077; fax 020 7633 9499

www.southwaterbooks.com; www.annesspublishing.com

Anness Publishing has a new picture agency outlet for images for
publishing, promotions or advertising. Please visit our website
www.practicalpictures.com for more information.

UK agent: The Manning Partnership Ltd; tel. 01225 478444;
fax 01225 478440; sales@manning-partnership.co.uk
UK distributor: Grantham Book Services Ltd; tel. 01476
541080; fax 01476 541061; orders@gbs.tbs-ltd.co.uk
North American agent/distributor: National Book Network;
tel. 301 459 3366; fax 301 429 5746; www.nbnbooks.com
Australian agent/distributor: Pan Macmillan Australia;
tel. 1300 135 113; fax 1300 135 103;
customer.service@macmillan.com.au
New Zealand agent/distributor: David Bateman Ltd;
tel. (09) 415 7664; fax (09) 415 889

Publisher: Joanna Lorenz
Managing Editor: Linda Fraser
Editor: Joy Wotton
Designer: Nigel Partridge
Jacket Designer: Adelle Morris
Illustrator: Peter Bull Art Studio
Production Controller: Claire Rae

ETHICAL TRADING POLICY
Because of our ongoing ecological investment programme, you,
as our customer, can have the pleasure and reassurance of
knowing that a tree is being cultivated on your behalf to
naturally replace the materials used to make the book you are
holding. For further information about this scheme, go to
www.annesspublishing.com/trees

Previously published as part of a larger volume,
The Rise and Fall of Ancient Rome

ACKNOWLEDGEMENTS

Ancient Art and Architecture Collection: 16b, 38t, 40t, 41b, 44t,
50b, 57b, 61t, 74t, 88t. **The Art Archive**: 8–9, 13t, 14, 15b, 17b,
21, 27t, 35b, 43t, 44b, 58t, 60t, 63b, 71t, 72t, 73, 83b, 84, 85b,
92–3, 96, 100b, 101, 103, 105, 107t, 109b, 114, 115b, 116t, 117,
119t, 120t, 124t, /Museo Prenestino Palestrina 24b, 26, /National
Archaeological Museum Chieti 13b, /National Museum Bucharest
18–19. **Bridgeman Art Library**: 51t, 59b, 68t, 106, 118t, 119b,
/Index 79, /Lauros Giraudon 62, 100t. **Colchester Museums**: 29.
Corbis: /Paul Almasy 66t, /Archivo Iconografico 20b, 22, 27b, 40b,
75, 82, 111, 121, 128t, /Nathan Benn 90b, /Bettmann 47b, 66b,
98t, /Michael Busselle 80b, Dean Conger 85t, /Robert Estall 31,
32t, /Shai Ginott 91t, /Jason Hawkes 68b, /Lindsay Hebberd 78b,
/Chris Hellier 125, /Historical Picture Archive 88b, /John Howard
Cordaiy Photo Library Ltd 112t, /Hanan Isachar 32b, /Bob Krist
67, /Paul H Kuiper 52t, /Charles & Josette Lenars 20t, 24t, 25, 43b,
56, 90t, 91b, /Araldo de Luca 15t, 16t, 28, 36–7, 50t, 54–5, 61b,
64, 128b, /Francis G Mayer 9, 39t, 94, /Michael Nicholson 33t,
/Richard T Nowitz 60b, /Dagli Orti 28b, /Polypix Eye Ubiquitous
113b, /Vittoriano Rastelli 33b, /Grant Smith 17t, /Roman Soumar
49t, /Vince Streano 112b, /Ruggero Vanni 11t, 48b, 102, 116b,
124b, /Vanni Archive 48t, 108b, 110t, /Sandro Vannini 71b, /Patrick
Ward 49b, 76–7, /K M Westermann 87t, /Nik Wheeler 41t, /Wild
Country 70, /Peter M Wilson 123b, /Roger Wood 6, 47t, 87b, 95t,
97, 110b, /Adam Woolfitt 34, 52b, 72b, 109t, 115t. **Dr Jon
Coulston**: 11b. **Dr Hazel Dodge**: 57t. **Mary Evans Picture Library**:
12, 69b, 118b. **www.miniatures.de<http://www.miniatures.de>**:
30, 81. **Scala, Florence**: 10, 35t, 38b, 39, 45t, 46, 74b, 78t, 80t,
83t, 89, 95b, 98b, 104, 107b, 120b, 122, 123t, 126, 127b.

Main jacket illustration: Mounted soldier in battle, 2nd century BC.
p. 1: A 3rd-century AD cavalry helmet.
p. 2: A Roman garrison on the River Nile.
p. 3: The siege of Alesia.
p. 4: The eagle of the legion.

CONTENTS

INTRODUCTION

The Romans called their empire imperium Romanorum. This translates rather appositely as the power of the Romans. For contemporaries, there was no escaping the military fact of Roman power. Subject peoples who incurred Rome's anger knew that the heavy weight of Rome's military machine could descend on them with exemplary efficiency.

AN INDOMITABLE FORCE

The Roman army was indisputably the best armed and most efficient military operation in the ancient world – at least in those areas it knew – although its navy was of minor importance. For a period of more than half a millennium, from the defeat of Hannibal in 202BC to Rome's own stunning defeat by the Goths at Adrianople in AD378, Rome was generally undefeated. Individual Roman generals could be outwitted or outmanoeuvred, and at the empire's extremities – in northern Britain, the deep forests of central Germany or the deserts of Asia – Rome's power seemed to reach its limits. But elsewhere, no other army could in the long term resist Roman military might; it was relentless, unflinching and genuinely invincible. Rome's army was not just the first fully professional army to operate on a global scale throughout the known world; for a very long time it was most probably the only such force deserving the name. Certainly Europe and the Middle East would not see such a force operating again until the 17th century at the earliest.

In many ways, Rome's example as a country-wide military power was not to be surpassed until the career of Napoleon Bonaparte at the turn of the 19th century. The "Little Emperor" from Corsica openly and repeatedly borrowed aspects of Roman power when creating his own militaristic empire with its eagles, arches and client states.

Above: Mars, the god of war, was appositely the god of the early Roman state, forever at war with its neighbours. Sacrifices were made to him by generals before they set out for battle, and after victory he received his share of booty.

Right: Hadrian's Wall, built in the far north of the Roman Empire, became its most imposing fortification. Stretching 76 miles (122km) from the River Tyne to the Solway, its eastern part was built in stone and its western part was built initially in turf.

The following text labels appear on the map:

BRITANNIA INFERIOR
BRITANNIA SUPERIOR
ATLANTIC OCEAN
GERMANIA INFERIOR
GERMANIA SUPERIOR
LUGDUNENSIS
BELGICA
RAETIA
AQUITANIA
NORICUM
PANNONIA INFERIOR
ALPES GRAIAE ET POENINAE
PANNONIA SUPERIOR
DACIA
BOSPORUS
NARBONENSIS
ALPES COTTIAE
MOESIA SUPERIOR
MOESIA INFERIOR
BLACK SEA
CASPIAN SEA
LUSITANIA
TARRACONENSIS
ALPES MARITIMAE
CORSICA
ITALIA
DALMATIA
THRACIA
BITHYNIA AND PONTUS
CAPPADOCIA
ARMENIA
BAETICA
SARDINIA
MACEDONIA
ASIA
GALATIA
MESOPOTAMIA
MAURETANIA TINGITANA
MAURETANIA CAESARIENSIS
SICILIA
EPIRUS
ACHAEA
LYCIA ET PAMPHYLIA
CILICIA
CYPRUS
SYRIA COELE
SYRIA PHOENICE
NUMIDIA
AFRICA PROCONSULARIS
MEDITERRANEAN SEA
SYRIA PALAESTINA
CRETA ET CYRENE
ARABIA
AEGYPTUS

ORDER IN THE RANKS

Above all, the Romans were remarkably disciplined soldiers. Rome, surrounded by land-hungry tribes, was frequently at war. Military discipline helped make the Romans a force to be reckoned with and keep them highly effective imperial rulers. Appropriately, Mars, god of war, was originally Rome's chief god. If its early wars were little more than glorified raids, when the Roman army grew larger it soon distinguished itself from other armies by its tenacity and readiness to innovate, taking what it needed from other people's customs and practices.

Under its first kings, the army of Rome consisted of individual warriors fighting mostly on foot, led by aristocrats. Roman infantrymen were primarily swordsmen. Rome did not acquire or keep its empire by noble ideals or fine words. It was, first and last, a nation of soldiers. Our word emperor comes from *imperator*, victorious commander-in-chief, for emperors were above all the supreme generals of Rome.

The triumphal arches the Romans erected around their empire celebrated bloody military victories. For a triumph, a general had to have killed at least 5,000 of the enemy. The Romans could be methodically brutal in their reprisals, literally razing the city of Carthage to the ground in 146BC, for example.

PAX ROMANA: THE ROMAN PEACE

It is easy to forget the benefits of external peace and internal security when they have become the accustomed way of life. Roman citizens knew their freedom and prosperity depended on military power and the *Pax Romana*, the Roman peace Augustus established and his successors long maintained.

What Rome's army gave the war-torn ancient world was unprecedented peace, security and stability for more than two centuries after Augustus reunited the empire in 30BC. Rome's wars of conquest were often undeniably brutal, but her enduring peace atoned for this in the end.

Above: The empire in AD200, centred on the Mediterranean, but stretching from the Middle East to Scotland.

Below: Carthage was brutally destroyed by the Roman army in 146BC, but rebuilt to rival Rome in magnificence.

CHAPTER I

THE PEOPLE'S ARMY

The growth of the Roman army, from an unpaid citizens' militia to a world-conquering professional force, made possible the growth of the Roman empire. The Roman army was Rome's greatest institution. The city, surrounded by enemies from the start, survived by taking the offensive. Two factors distinguished the Roman army in its long prime from the mid-4th century BC until after AD200: flexibility and tenacity. As the long, often catastrophic war against Hannibal (218–202BC) showed, panic was a Greek word seldom found in a Roman's vocabulary. In the later Republic, almost constant wars turned a part-time self-defence force into a full-time army. Deficiencies, revealed in wars in Africa, called for radical reforms provided by Marius, who opened the army to the poorest citizens as a career. From 100BC the army became fully professional and under the Principate was paid by the *princeps*. In return, soldiers swore allegiance to the *princeps*. Military and civilian careers long remained intertwined. Young Roman nobles served in the army before starting political careers, retaining vital links between civilian and military life. But from the mid-3rd century AD on, soldiers and civilians were segregated by emperors to prevent revolts. Disarmed, the citizens grew ever more timid, while soldiers became more detached from, and openly contemptuous of, the civilians whose taxes supported them and whose lives they supposedly were protecting.

Left: Officers and soldiers of the Praetorian guard, the elite imperial bodyguard stationed in Rome.

BATTLE HARDENING

King Pyrrhus was astonished less by his defeat at the hands of a non-Greek city, than by the Romans' refusal to accept the rules of war as then understood by Greeks. By the 3rd century BC, these had become relatively civilized. Wars were fought between mercenaries, who were not expected to fight to the last drop of blood. By contrast, the disciplined Romans (who Pyrrhus acknowledged were "not barbarians"), fought with grim determination both on the battlefield and in the political arena. Rome would tolerate high casualties in its citizen armies, but would accept no compromise treaties with enemies strong enough to recover and possibly challenge her again. Unconditional surrender or total destruction was the choice offered to rival powers. This might be brutal, but it proved devastatingly effective.

When Rome and Carthage went to war in 264BC, Rome had no fleet to combat the Mediterranean's greatest maritime power. Carthage's wealth enabled her to hire huge armies of mercenaries. The Romans, however, set about building a

Below: Only in the First Punic War did the Roman fleet play a crucial role. Thanks to the corvus, *which bound ships together, Rome defeated Carthage repeatedly at sea.*

fleet for what proved to be a naval war. Wars at sea were fought by galleys, rowed by oarsmen. The Romans copied a Carthaginian galley that had run aground, training rowing crews – poorer citizens – on land while they built 140 cloned ships. The first naval clash proved a disaster, and the Romans realized that they could not out-manoeuvre the experienced Carthaginians. Instead, they devised the *corvus*, or raven, a boarding ramp with an iron spike that fell and stuck into the enemy's deck, locking the two galleys together. Naval skills became redundant as Roman legionaries charged across and got down to hand-to-hand combat.

At the Battle of Mylae in 260BC, a larger Carthaginian fleet was totally defeated, losing 50 ships including its flagship thanks to this unnautical novelty. The Romans defeated the Carthaginians again in 256BC at Ecnomus. The Romans went on the offensive, landing an army under Regulus in North Africa. However, Regulus was defeated in 255BC and taken prisoner. A relief fleet was sunk by a storm, as were other fleets because the corvus made galleys top-heavy. Finally, the Romans raised another fleet and won the decisive battle of the Aegates Islands in 242BC. Carthage gave up Sicily and her fleet. Her ruling families, like the Barcas, however, were determined on revenge.

ENDURANCE AND INNOVATION

In Hannibal Barca, Rome encountered a military genius. Hannibal recruited his army from the best fighting nations – Numidian cavalry, Spanish and Celtic infantry. Against such a force, Rome fielded its superior militia. Rome still carried out a fresh mobilization each year, and still appointed amateur generals from that year's consuls. Rome's only obvious strength was the huge supply of recruits from her allied cities – 700,000 men.

Hannibal's three swift victories – at Trebbia, Trasimene and, most devastatingly, at Cannae in 216BC – should have won the war. But they were not cheap victories: Cannae cost Hannibal 5,700 men. The Roman maniples' triple lines helped soldiers to keep fighting even in defeat. So did their discipline. Rome, with its belief in its gods, fought on. Although it might have seemed wiser to keep troops at home, legions were sent to Spain. Fabius Maximus wore Hannibal down by avoiding open battle and reconquering the south. The long sieges of Capua, Tarento and Syracuse showed Roman inventiveness at its best. Scipio took the offensive in Spain, adopting Hannibal's own tactics (placing heavy legions on the wings with light troops in the centre) to crush the Carthaginians at Ilipa in 206BC. He then defeated Hannibal at Zama in 202BC, where the Romans outfought the Carthaginians, after turning back their elephants.

Above: The scene from the Temple of Neptune in Rome c.100BC shows soldiers of the late Republic equipped with long shields, plumed helmets and, for the officer by the altar, a cuirass. Soon after this time, Roman soldiers stopped providing their own armour.

Below: Roman troops cross water using a bridge of boats.

THE FALL OF THE REPUBLIC

Success can breed complacency, as Rome discovered in the later 2nd century BC, when it struggled against adversaries who were often less formidable than those it had already overcome. The army's lack of full professional status was one of the main problems. Essentially, most Roman soldiers still expected to return to their farms at the end of a campaign – although these were usually ruined by often long periods of absence. This left many men without property, making them and their sons ineligible for further military service, and so weakening the army. These shortcomings were corrected by Marius' army reforms. In the long term, these proved fatal to the Republic's existence.

Military problems first became apparent in the Third Punic War (149–146BC). Disturbed by Carthage's economic – not military – resurgence, Rome engineered war after Carthage became entangled with its aggressive neighbour Numidia, officially breaking its treaty with Rome. The Roman armies suffered repeated reverses until Scipio Aemilianus (the adopted grandson of Scipio Africanus) took command and stormed Carthage, destroying the city.

Worse followed in Spain, where Iberian tribes fought each other and Rome endlessly. Another revolt against Rome, based in the northern city of Numantia, proved intractable. Untrained Roman armies were defeated until Scipio assembled and trained an army of 60,000 men. Even then, he did not dare face the Numantians in open battle but used siege tactics to capture and destroy their city in 133BC. Such brutality had become a hallmark of Roman imperialism but was now coupled with military semi-competence.

Back in Africa, another challenge to Roman power arose with Jugurtha, a fine general and king of Numidia (northern Algeria). He defeated a Roman army in 110BC, forcing it to "pass under the yoke". He proved so successful at eluding superior Roman armies that treachery was suspected. Roman troops deserted in droves, as their commanders appeared incompetent or corrupt. The arrival of the martinet Quintus Metellus restored discipline and morale, but he failed to catch Jugurtha. Impatient for a successful conclusion, the Roman Assembly chose Marius, a *novus homo*, or "new man", from an equestrian family.

MARIUS AND HIS REFORMS

After serving under Metellus as consul in 107BC, Marius was given the African command the next year. Before leaving Rome, he appealed for volunteers from the propertyless class, the *capite censi*, helping to turn a citizens' militia into a career army that appealed to landless poorer citizens. With a much increased supply of recruits, Marius won victories in Africa that revealed his own military talents. But he failed to corner Jugurtha until treachery led to his capture and final execution in Rome in 104BC.

Meanwhile in the north, two large Germanic peoples, the Cimbri and the Teutones, annihilated twin Roman armies at Arausio (Orange) in 105BC. In the

Above: A standard of a cohort, the subdivision of the legion.

Below: Lepidus, Mark Antony and Octavian formed the Second Triumvirate in 43BC.

worst disaster since Cannae, 80,000 men were reported lost. Marius was again given command by the Assembly and in three years radically restructured the army.

The three lines based on experience and age were abolished. All legionaries now had a *pilum* (javelin) plus the short *gladius* (sword) and had to carry supplies on their backs, hence the new nickname "Marius' mules". The basic sub-unit became the cohort of 480 men, which was divided into six centuries of 80 men each commanded by a centurion, officers who became the backbone of the army. Each legion had its own standard, a gilt eagle, that embodied the legion's *esprit de corps*. The legions themselves became more permanent, and, most importantly, these full-time legionaries started looking to their generals for reward, the Senate having failed to look after its demobilized soldiers.

This new-style army proved far more flexible than its predecessor. Marius used his uniformly equipped cohorts to crush the Teutones in a bloody battle at Aix-en-Provence in 102BC and the next year to rout the Cimbri in northern Italy, reportedly killing 100,000 of them. The most alarming barbarian invasions until the 3rd century AD had been repelled and Marius was (unconstitutionally) re-elected consul yet again.

THE RESULTS OF THE REFORMS

After Marius, no one won supreme power in Rome (as opposed to just becoming consul) without an army to back him. Powerful Roman generals – first Marius, then Sulla, Pompey, Caesar, and finally Antony and Octavian – built up armies that were loyal to them rather than to the state, and could use them for personal reasons. Sulla, once Marius' lieutenant in Africa, led the army he had been assigned for war against Mithradates against Rome itself in 88BC, the first of many such "marches on Rome". From Marius' reforms until the end of the Republic, Rome's armies were used against each other almost as much as against foreign enemies. This wrecked the Republic.

The *military* consequences of Marius' reforms were almost wholly positive, however. The Social War with the Latin allies of 91–87BC had given the allies Roman citizenship and greatly increased the numbers eligible for legionary service. These professional legions made a superb permanent army. Reorganized and supplemented by increasing numbers of specialized auxiliaries – from Balearic slingers to African cavalry – they continued Rome's conquest of the ancient world, successfully defending it until the mid-3rd century AD with only minor changes in their structure.

Below: The eagle-standard introduced by Marius became the focus of loyalty among legionaries. To lose one in battle was a disgrace, and the aquilifer, eagle-bearer, was an important soldier. But loyalty to the legion did not always mean loyalty to the Republic.

LEGIONS AND PRINCIPATE

Above: A legionary of the 1st century BC with his pilum *(javelin) and* gladius *(sword).*

When Octavian, victorious after the lengthy civil wars, returned to Rome in 29BC, a pressing problem was how to deal with a huge army of nearly 70 legions, plus a large fleet. Such swollen forces were unsustainable by an empire exhausted economically, and unnecessary when Rome faced no major external threats. They also posed a potential future threat to the stability of his regime should they become loyal to a successful and ambitious general. Although Octavian had risen to power by the sword, he did not wish to advertise the fact. Above all, he wanted to ensure the loyalty of the army to himself and later to his family, to avert any recurrence of civil war.

Octavian decided on demobilization, reducing the army's size to only 28 legions (around 150,000 regular soldiers). This meant that he needed to find a way of paying off some 300,000 veterans with grants of land in ways that did not anger too many existing landholders. Augustus, as he was titled from 27BC, did this by founding colonies of veterans, often outside Italy – in Spain, Sicily, Gaul, Greece, Syria and Pisidia (central Turkey). He also established 28 colonies in Italy, some of which became famous in his lifetime. Turin is a good example. His vast wealth allowed him to pay fair prices for land in Italy. The revenues of Egypt flowed directly into the imperial purse and he owned vast tracts of land taken from enemies. In AD6 Augustus set up the *Aerarium militare*, a special military treasury, to meet legionaries' retirement pensions from indirect taxes.

The 28 legions – reduced to 25 after the Teutoburg disaster – were stationed in troubled provinces such as Tarraconensis (northern Spain) and along the frontiers, especially the Rhine and Danube, where permanent fortresses were established, later to develop into towns such as Cologne or Vienna. The Rhine was the early crucial frontier, with eight legions stationed along it, some in double camps such as Xanten. Later, the Danube became the most important. Under the Principate, legions were commanded by legates, who held delegated power (*imperium*) from Augustus. He kept only nine cohorts of the elite Praetorian guard in Italy and stationed only three of them in Rome – a tiny military force for a city of nearly a million inhabitants. Along the frontiers, the lower-paid, more lightly armed auxiliaries, recruited from non-Roman citizens, supplemented the legions.

This frontier deployment meant that there was no central reserve, at least until Septimius Severus (AD193–211) based a legion near Rome. Although criticisms

Left: Legionaries of the Principate, with curved shields, lorica segmantata *armour, short swords and* pilum, *the javelin with the thin neck.*

Right: A Roman centurion as imagined in the Italian Renaissance, with his sword on his left and wearing ornate armour.

have been levelled against Augustus for this lack, in practice it probably made little difference given the length of the frontiers and the slow progress of marching legionaries . The army remained *potentially* on the offensive, ready to move along or across the frontiers. A central reserve under an ambitious commander might also prove a threat to the emperor. Augustus did establish three fleets to keep the Mediterranean free of pirates as well as flotillas on the Rhine, Danube and Nile, but naval power was always secondary to land power.

LOYALTY TO THE *PRINCEPS*

All new recruits swore a *sacramentum*, or oath to the *princeps*, rather than to the Senate. But, unlike Caesar or Pompey, Augustus was not a great general. He owed his earlier victories (over Sextus Pompeius and Antony) principally to Marcus Agrippa, his chief minister and closest ally. After Actium, Augustus campaigned only in northern Spain in 23BC. He fell seriously ill there and seldom again took the field, but troops did not swear allegiance to the general Agrippa. The image of the emperor or of one of his family was carried by an *imaginifer*, a standard-bearer ranking behind only the *aquilifer*, the eagle-bearer. The emperor's name was coupled with that of *Roma Dea* (Rome the goddess) in sacrifices and his image appeared on busts and coins. Such reiterated expressions of loyalty to the *imperator* or Caesar, helped to cement Augustus' settlement, enabling it to survive the antics of Caligula and even, for a surprisingly long time, those of Nero. Nero's almost total neglect of the military was a major cause of his downfall.

Augustus was fortunate that in his stepsons Drusus and especially Tiberius (from AD6 his adopted son) he had extremely competent generals who campaigned steadily on the Rhine and

Danube. Their military successes reflected on the *princeps*. Later emperors were less lucky but faced few serious challenges from army commanders until AD68 and the Year of the Four Emperors. Thereafter, dynastic continuity, coupled with generous donations at each emperor's accession, helped to keep the legions loyal. When a general did revolt, like Saturninus in AD89, he was quickly quashed. This contributed to the success both of the Flavians and of the Five Good Emperors – all of the latter being adopted sons. Ironically, when Marcus Aurelius made Commodus (whom he believed to be his actual son) his heir, the dynasty came to an end and the ensuing civil wars, longer and more damaging than in AD68–9, weakened the empire.

Below: The imperial guard as they appear on the base of the Obelisk of Theodosius I, a 4th-century AD emperor, in Constantinople (Istanbul).

ARMY OF THE LATER EMPIRE

During the mid-3rd-century AD crisis, it became obvious that the traditional deployment of the army had become inadequate. Withdrawing legions from one frontier to fight on another left the exposed frontier intolerably vulnerable. The persistent and well-organized Sassanid Persians were more deadly than the earlier Parthians. The Germanic Goths, who first appeared on the Danube delta in AD242, were also formidable. Over the next 30 years they penetrated into the empire's Mediterranean heart, sometimes seizing ships. Athens, far from any frontier, was sacked in AD268 by the Heruli, another tribe that was wandering the empire almost at will.

At least 30 emperors held power between the murder of Alexander Severus in AD235, and AD284, the accession of Diocletian. Only one died a natural death (Claudius Gothicus in AD270). Many more usurpers were acclaimed by mutinous legions throughout the empire. A few, like Postumus in Gaul and Carausius in Britain, formed breakaway empires that lasted years. The lack of a central reserve and the intertwining of civilian and military careers now appeared terrible weaknesses.

Around AD200, Septimius Severus had begun building a reserve in Italy, doubling the Praetorian guard and stationing a legion near Rome. This created a mobile force of around 18,000 men. Later, Gallienus (AD253–68) banned senators from holding senior commands and began building up a mobile cavalry force in northern Italy, drawing on *vexillationes* (detachments). Like his removal of the government to Milan, close to the Alpine passes and the Rhine–Danube frontiers, this concentration of forces around the emperor set a precedent. Gallienus was murdered before he could employ this force to lasting effect, but his successors, Claudius II and Aurelian (AD270–75), used it to defeat the Goths, Palmyrene rebels and the separatist Gallic empire. Aurelian also accelerated the programme of refortifying cities, notably the capital itself. These steps marked the start of a radical change in tactics and strategy that was completed by Constantine.

CRACK TROOPS – AND THE REST

Constantine (AD324–37) continued to make the army more mobile, dividing it into two groups that were distinct in armour, pay, prestige and role. The low-paid *limitanei* were the frontier guards and the elite *comitatenses* were mobile forces grouped around the emperors. The latter were often cavalry: scale-armoured *cataphracts* or *clibanarii* with plate armour. Such horsemen looked imposing but were often ineffectual. Julian had to discipline cavalry units for cowardice during his Persian campaign in AD363 and the indiscipline of Valens' cavalry was partly responsible for his defeat at Adrianople in AD378. Before the widespread adoption of the stirrup – now known not to have occurred much before AD600 – heavy cavalry was of limited use, for lances could not be used in charges. The impact of hitting an opponent would have unseated a stirrupless rider.

Above: Light-armed auxiliary troops, with clubs but no armour, supplement the legionaries on this detail from Trajan's Column in Rome.

Below: The massive walls of Richborough, Rome's chief port of entry to Britain and part of the Saxon Shore defences of the 3rd century AD, show the empire was on the defensive.

FORTIFICATIONS PROGRAMME
To protect the vulnerable cities of the interior, new fortresses or fortified towns – known as *burgi*, a German word – became nodal strong points, usually invulnerable to direct attack by barbarians. At York, old walls were replaced by thick defensive walls capable of carrying pieces of artillery. This huge fortification programme was replicated across the empire. Behind these huge walls, frontier troops could await the arrival of the mobile relief forces. Large landowners began fortifying their villas or farms, so that invaders, even if undefeated in the field, would face starvation outside the walls.

Constantine created *palatini*, imperial Palatine guards, to replace the Praetorians. Many of these were German horsemen. This increasing dependence on Germanic mercenaries is symbolized by the adoption of "dragon standards" – long, wind-sock-style banners – and German war cries. By AD379, when Theodosius became emperor after Adrianople, the Goths had become *foederati*, or allies, with whole tribes enrolled *en masse*. When imperial government divided after Theodosius' death in AD395, the Goths turned against their Roman allies and started the chain of events that led to the sack of Rome in AD410.

The empire in the 4th century AD still had about 60 legions, each now made up of only about 1,000 lightly armed men. The infantry no longer wore much body armour and used darts rather than the *pilum* (javelin). Nonetheless, properly led and trained Roman armies could still defeat their enemies, as victorious campaigns from Galerius' victory over the Persians in AD297 to Valentinian's campaigns against the Germans in the AD360s showed. Often, however, Rome's armies were deployed against each other.

The *limitanei*, stationary frontier troops garrisoning the new forts, were unimpressive. Many were expected to grow their own food, as they were not paid all year round. Nonetheless, some of these frontier troops continued to fight for the western empire right up to the end in the AD470s. In AD534, after the eastern empire had reconquered North Africa, the emperor Justinian ordered the re-establishment of the *limitanei* to defend the long frontiers. But the actual reconquest of the west – Africa, Italy, southern Spain – was carried out by smallish numbers of cavalry. An army of 20,000 men was by then thought large.

How effective the army of the later empire was is debatable, but it was certainly more expensive, and the taxes to pay for it contributed to the alienation of subjects from the imperial government. But as Roman civilians were increasingly loath to fight – there are reports of men of military age mutilating themselves to avoid conscription under Constantine – there seemed little alternative. The continued survival of the eastern empire, and its 6th-century revival, suggests that the late-Roman army could fight effectively at least at times.

Above: York was for long a legionary headquarters and the capital of northern Britain. Two emperors – Septimius Severus and Constantius Chlorus – died in the city, and Constantine I was proclaimed emperor there by his troops.

Below: This scene from the Arch of Galerius in Thessalonica, Greece, commemorates Galerius' victory over the Persians in AD297. Elephants, often used by the Persians, can just be glimpsed in the background.

CHAPTER II

INSIDE
THE ARMY

As the Roman army became a world-conquering force, it evolved an original system of organization. Based on the legion, this model had the flexibility to overcome much larger, and often technically superior, enemy forces. Above all, it was indomitably aggressive. From the earliest wars of the Republic in the 5th century BC up to the 3rd century AD, its core troops were the legionaries: highly disciplined, well-armoured, heavy infantry-men who could fight in many different ways, from storming fortresses to outfacing charging elephants or even, as marines, fighting onboard ships.

The Roman army was notorious for its tough discipline and rigorous demands. However, for its age it was also oddly meritocratic, and in some ways continued to represent the voice of the Roman people after the Republic had ended. In effect, it spoke, as well as fought, for the people of the whole empire, not just Rome. The legions were often remarkably long-lived – some units lasted more than 300 years. In so doing, they became the unwitting agents of a process of Romanization that transformed western Europe through the towns that sprang up around their camps, or in the peaceful hinterland guarded by them. Many of the bridges, aqueducts and walls around the former provinces were built by legionaries in the long periods of peace that their fighting had established. The Roman army was more than just an army: in some ways it became the heart of Rome itself.

Left: Legionaries, besides being professional soldiers, often also became skilled builders, constructing many forts and roads.

ORGANIZING THE LEGION

Above: A Roman optio, *the second-in-command to a centurion, with his distinctive plumed helmet, worn by a member of the re-enactment group the Ermine St Guard. Officers such as the* optio *and the centurion were the army's backbone, and they received higher pay.*

Below: The symbol of the 20th Roman legion, Valeria Victrix.

Legio means levy, and originally a legion was the levy of all eligible Roman citizens between the ages of 17 and 46, arranged in centuries (literally 100 men). The Roman army of around 500BC numbered around 4,000–6,000 men, hoplite heavy spearmen, like the Greeks. Over the next centuries, however, the legion proper emerged as a new, more adaptable unit that enabled Rome to conquer and hold the Mediterranean world.

By *c.*320BC, the legion of the Republic had been established. According to Polybius and Livy – who do not always agree – a legion had five elements: cavalry, light infantry and three sorts of heavy infantry. The richest citizens made up the cavalry of about 300 men, socially prestigious but too few to affect battles. The all-important heavy infantry, about 4,200 men who could afford their own armour, was divided into three lines. The first line had the youngest soldiers, the *hastati* (literally "armed with a spear", although they carried javelins and swords). Next came the *principes*, men in their prime, and last came the *triarii*, the veterans. Behind the *triarii* were deployed less dependable troops, *rorarii* and *accensi*. All soldiers wore bronze helmets and had a long shield of wood covered with leather. The *hastati* and *principes* were armed with the *pilum*, or javelin, and the *gladius*, or short sword, about 20in (50cm) long. The *triarii* appear to have had longer spears. The *velites* were light infantry too poor to equip themselves with full armour.

All three lines were organized into ten maniples. This, the smallest fighting unit, had two centuries, commanded by the senior centurion. Maniples of the *hastati* and *principes* numbered about 120–60 men each, while the *triarii* made up ten maniples of about 60 men. Each maniple also had about 40 *velites*, or lightly armed troops. In battle, the maniples were arranged in the *triplex acies* (triple battle-order) of a chequerboard formation. The maniples of the *principes* covered the gaps between those of the *hastati*, and their own gaps were covered by those of the *triarii*. The *velites* seem to have been used as skirmishers. Each legion of Roman citizens was augmented by an equal number of allies (about 4,000–5,000 infantry and 900 cavalry), commanded by Roman officers. These were called *alae* (wings) because in battle they were put on the wings of the main legions.

The *triplex acies* proved its virtues by defeating the numerically and technically superior armies of Pyrrhus, the Macedonians and the Seleucids. The flexibility and discipline of the maniples – opening up to let hostile elephants or cavalry through, for example – was very nearly invincible. When the Romans were defeated, notably by Hannibal, it was due to Roman amateurism, for the armies were disbanded after each campaign and had to be recruited afresh. When armies remained in existence for a long time under a great general such as Scipio Africanus, they were superb, as the run of Roman victories from Zama in 202BC to Pydna in 168BC showed.

THE CLASSIC LEGION
Rome's military reputation was dented by defeats in the later 2nd century BC, which culminated in disaster at Arausio (Orange). Twin armies were annihilated by the Cimbri and Teutones in 105BC with the loss of 80,000 men. Such a defeat led Marius, recently emerged as the people's general in the war against Jugurtha, to reorganize the legion radically. He had already abolished the property qualifications. Now he got rid of all distinctions based on class or age: both the *velites* and the cavalry disappeared. All legionaries were identically armed with the *pilum* and *gladius*, and had mail armour and a long shield. The maniples ceased to be the

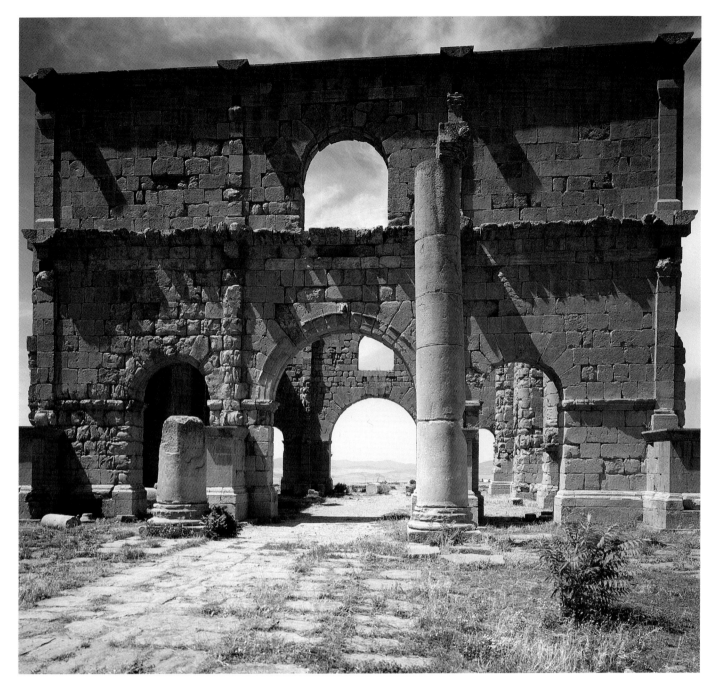

basic unit, although they remained in existence for a while. Instead, the chief tactical sub-unit became the cohort, ten of which made up a legion.

Each cohort had about 480 men divided into six centuries of 80 men led by a centurion. Later the first cohort was usually double strength, raising a legion's total strength to 5,280 men. *Alae*, no longer allies but cavalry wings recruited from auxiliaries, were specialist, increasingly well-regarded units either 512- or 768-men strong. Ten cohorts were easier to command than 30 maniples and could be deployed as wanted. The cohort did not command the same loyalty as the century and the legion. Marius introduced the silver (later gilt) *aquila*, or eagle, as each legion's main standard, symbolizing its pride and identity. Legions now became permanent, offering a career to landless citizens who volunteered. These became highly professional soldiers, who looked to their generals for substantial reward after their service. This had huge political as well as military consequences.

Above: The principia, headquarters, at the legionary fort of Lambaesis (Tazoult) in modern-day Algeria.

CENTURIONS AND OFFICERS

Centurions may be seen as the equivalent of sergeant-majors in the modern British army. Yet they were even more important, effectively ranking between a contemporary captain and a major. Beside them, a legion's senatorial officers and commander could appear semi-skilled amateurs.

Centurions needed to be not only excellent soldiers but literate, for they had to read and write orders and could have political or diplomatic roles. A letter of introduction from someone influential helped one become a centurion; in the Roman army, as in the Roman state, personal connections counted for a lot. Former members of the Praetorian guard in Rome and, more rarely, equestrians applied for centurions' posts. But some centurions rose from the ranks of the legion, staying 40 years in the army.

There were 59 centurions in a legion, one for each ordinary century of 80 men in the normal nine cohorts and (from c.50AD on), five for the first cohort of five double centuries. This cohort's centurions, the most senior in the legion, were known as *primi ordines*, of the first rank. In ascending order these were the *hastatus posterior* (a name recalling the extinct *maniples*), the *princeps posterior, hastatus, princeps* and *primus pilus*. The *primus pilus* was the most important officer in the whole legion. He had to be at least 50 years old and held his post for only a year, after which he might retire, his gratuity of 400–600,000 sesterces elevating him to equestrian rank. (A normal legionary received about 3,000 sesterces on retirement under Augustus.) Some went on to become

Above: The most vital of officers in the Roman army, a centurion was colourfully, even resplendently, armoured, with crested helmet and medallioned cuirass. Note the vine branch in his right hand – used for beating his men.

Right: This tombstone commemorates the centurion Marcus Caelius of the Eighteenth Legion, who was killed fighting at the age of 53 in the Teutoburg Forest ambush in Germany in AD9.

prefect of the camp, another very important post, others became *primus pilus* again, adding *bis* or *ter* (second or third) to their title; a few became provincial governors or fleet commanders; one or two even became prefects of the Praetorian guard.

A centurion was distinguishable by his silvered armour, his greaves (shin armour, also worn by legionaries) and his transverse-crested helmet. He wore his sword on his left and his dagger on the right, but still carried a shield. Centurions were responsible for maintaining Roman discipline, using their *vitis* (vine cane) often to ferocious effect on their men. This could make them very unpopular. One centurion was killed by angry legionaries during the mutiny on the Danube in AD14. He was known as *cedo alterum* (Get me another!) due to his habit of beating soldiers until his cane broke. Centurions often took bribes from their men, for granting leave or exempting them from fatigues. But they paid for their privileges in blood, suffering disproportionately high casualties in battle, as they were expected to stand their ground to the end.

Beneath the centurions were the standard-bearers: the *aquilifer* (the eagle-bearer), the *signifer* (the emperor's image-bearer) – who also looked after soldiers' pay and savings – and the *vexillarius*, (legionary standard-bearer). All were important posts, especially the *aquilifer*. When Caesar's troops hesitated before disembarking on the shores of Britain, the *aquilifer* leapt into the water shouting, "Follow me, comrades!" And they did. Like these officers, the *optio*, the second-in-command of each century, was on double pay. Each century also had a *tesserarius*, responsible for the important sentry rota, and a *librarius* (clerk). At legionary headquarters there was a staff of clerks and orderlies, including the *exactores* (exactors of payments) and clerks with special duties such as the *librarii horreorum* (clerk of the granary records).

OTHER OFFICERS

The other officers in a legion, although theoretically senior, were less professional. Each legion had six tribunes, the senior being a *laticlavus*; the broad stripe on his toga indicated he was accepted for the Senate. He would be under 25, having his first military experience for a year or so before returning to civilian life. The other five tribunes, *angusticlavii*, or narrow stripes, came from the equestrian order and were generally older and far more experienced. They had often commanded an auxiliary cohort already. They had general administrative duties and, if competent, might go on to command large *alae* (500 or 1,000 men) of auxiliary cavalry. The commanding officer, the *legatus legionis*, was a senator in his 30s or 40s, appointed by the emperor and serving for three years. He might have had no military experience since serving as tribune long before. He was sometimes also the provincial governor. A legate relied heavily on his *primus pilus* and camp prefect for advice, but, as Varus in the Teutoburg ambush in AD9 showed, amateurish legates could not always be relied on to make sound military judgement in crises.

Above: Disciplined Roman swordmanship – stabbing more often than cutting – was a vital part of repeated Roman successes often against vastly superior numbers of barbarians. Better armour also played a part in Roman victories, although single combat like this was uncommon.

TRAINING AND DISCIPLINE

Above: Re-enactment of combat by Roman legionaries. In full armour, they are using their swords, the short but (in the right hands) lethal gladius.

What most impressed foreign commentators about the Roman army was its exceptional discipline and training. Their battle drills were like war. "It would be fair enough to call their drills bloodless battles and their battles bloody drills" wrote Josephus, the captured Jewish leader who became a Roman citizen in AD67. Training and discipline were what made Roman armies so often victorious, not superiority in arms or numbers. When this combination began to break down in the 4th century AD, the army too began to disintegrate.

Every new recruit swore a *sacramentum* (oath) to his general, by which he abrogated all his civilian rights for his 26 years of service. The oath was renewed every year. From then on, his life was in the army's hands. According to Vegetius, writing on military affairs around AD400, a recruit was taught how to march in step and keep his place in formation. Regular route marches of 20 Roman miles (*c.*30km) in five hours, and of 24 miles (*c.*36 km) in the same time at quick step, helped to get a recruit fit.

Drilled twice a day, he learnt how to vault on to a horse and how to mount and dismount fully armed from either side. He was taught to use his weapons by practising cuts and thrusts against a man-sized wooden stake. Initially, he used a heavy wooden sword and shield to strengthen his muscles. He would then fence with other recruits, the tip of his sword covered, before entire units waged mock battles against each other. The climax of such contests came with the mock-cavalry battles, the *hippaka gymnasia*, which were among the army's grandest spectacles. But above all, he was taught how to fight in formation without panicking, becoming so drilled in such discipline that it became second nature.

Training was not restricted to new recruits or to wartime. Repeated drilling kept the army at the peak of efficiency. The legionary was also taught other skills, including swimming, slinging and pitching camp. From *c.*100BC specialist sub-officers in each legion learnt more technical skills, such as building roads. All these were designed to produce an adaptable, tough, reliable soldier, skilled in swordsmanship and adept at keeping formation under exacting circumstances, and always obedient to military discipline.

Left: A Roman garrison on the River Nile from a 1st-century BC *mosaic. Egypt was one of the empire's softest postings.*

PUNISHMENTS AND REWARD

Death was the punishment for a wide range of offences: dereliction of guard duty (by falling asleep or going absent without leave), desertion, theft (from a comrade), perjury, homosexual acts with another soldier and cowardice. After a brief trial, the guilty soldier was hit with a staff by the tribune, a cue for the other soldiers to club or stone him to death. If he did not die at once, he was thrown outside the camp and abandoned. If an entire unit was found guilty of cowardice or mutiny, it might be decimated. Every tenth man, chosen by lot, would be bludgeoned to death and the remainder of the unit disgraced, pitching their tents outside the main camp and being fed barley rather than wheat. But there were other, less severe and probably more common types of punishment: reduction in rank, loss of privileges gained over years of service, corporal punishment and discharge with ignominy and no gratuity.

The Roman army did not rule solely by punishment; it offered rewards too. Booty from a successful campaign would be shared among the soldiers – although this obviously dwindled during peacetime – and there were occasional individual donations to worthy soldiers. The army also handed out military decorations such as silver or gold chains and *phalerae*

(medallions) of bronze or gold worn on the breastplate. Various *coronae* (crowns) were also awarded: the *corona civica* for personally saving the life of a Roman in battle, the *corona muralis* for the soldier who first scaled an enemy city's wall and the *corona vallaris* for the first to cross the entrenchment of an enemy fort. Under inspired generals, competition for such prizes could be intense and were sometimes shared, as at Cartagena in 210BC. From the time of Vespasian on, legionaries could also expect a donation from a new emperor on his accession.

Above: A modern-day re-enactment of Roman legionaries forming a testudo, *or tortoise shield roof, used when approaching walls. The discipline required to maintain such formations – it was said to be possible to walk on the locked shields – was learnt painfully during long army training.*

Left: A Roman legionary's training centred above all on learning how to use his gladius *(stabbing sword) to devastating effect. He would start with a wooden sword, which he jabbed at a pole, before progressing to a real iron weapon.*

PAY AND CONDITIONS

Above: Emperor Caracalla, who twice raised the soldiers' pay in the 3rd century AD.

Below: The Palestrina mosaic from the late 1st century BC shows soldiers, perhaps in a scene from a romantic myth.

Nobody could call the ordinary legionary of the Principate overpaid or pampered. After 26 years' service, he received a gratuity in land (not always where he wanted it) or in cash. This came to 3,000 denarii under Augustus and had only increased to 5,000 under Caracalla 200 years later. For most soldiers, yearly pay was also modest. According to Suetonius, Caesar doubled the pay of rank-and-file legionaries to 225 denarii a year in 49BC at the start of the Civil War, to keep them loyal. Basic pay remained at this rate until Domitian (AD81–96) raised it to 300 denarii. It then stayed unchanged throughout the 2nd century AD, despite steady inflation, until Septimius Severus and then Caracalla raised it twice early in the 3rd century AD. During that century,

rocketing inflation devalued the currency. The government responded by paying soldiers in kind – often letting them seize goods from civilians – or in gold currency, which alone retained its value.

Pay rose less with seniority than with promotion. According to Vegetius, a *tesserarius* received one-and-a-half times a normal legionary's pay, an *optio* twice and so on up the scale to centurions, the most junior of whom received at least five times the basic pay. The elite Praetorians were paid twice the basic rate, auxiliaries only half, although some cavalry *alae* (detachments) probably received at least as much as ordinary legionaries.

Supplementing the legionaries' annual pay were the *donativi*, or largesse, that most emperors gave out after their accession, or after a great – or purported – victory. Caligula, for example, gave all legionaries an extra four gold pieces (100 denarii) after his abortive "invasion" of Britain. Although weaker emperors undoubtedly resorted to bribery – according to Suetonius, Claudius gave the Praetorians who had spared his life 150 gold pieces (3,750 denarii) each – even Augustus left 75 denarii to each soldier in his will.

Out of their meagre pay, legionaries had to buy clothes, food, weapons and tents as well as bribes for the centurion. One of the centurion's chief perks was indeed taking bribes in return for granting leave or exemption from fatigues (chores), a practice that disciplinarians like the emperor Hadrian tried to stamp out. Discontent seems to have been widespread in AD14: Germanicus was almost killed stopping a mutiny among the Rhineland legionaries who had been engaged in campaigns for many years.

For food, Vegetius lists as staples corn, wine, vinegar and salt in plenty at all times. The men mostly ate porridge, bread and beans, supplemented by other vegetables and eggs, with meat on the numerous feast days, plus any obtained by hunting. When campaigning they ate hardtack, long-lasting wholewheat biscuits. Such hardships were made more acceptable by the way many generals, even those from the imperial family such as Tiberius or Julian, shared their troops' hardships while on campaign, sleeping on the ground and eating basic rations.

At first under Augustus, legionaries slept in simple timber huts or even in their leather tents. Soon, however, proper stone fortresses were built, often with amphitheatres just outside and with baths within or nearby. Bathhouses were regarded as absolutely essential, and the remains of a typically impressive one on a basilican plan have been found at Chester. Even more impressive are the baths at Caerleon, the largest military baths in Britain. The amphitheatres, in contrast,normally made of turf and timber in northern Europe, seldom saw full-scale gladiatorial games (since these were too expensive) but were used for festivals and animal displays.

Townships soon sprang up outside the larger camps, where men off duty could go to eat and drink in *tabernae* (taverns), and, of course, to meet women. These settlements (*canabae*) often grew into sizeable towns and a few became *coloniae*. But legionaries, although they often started and supported their own families, were not allowed to marry legally while on service until the reign of Septimius Severus. However, their partners were often recognized by people around them and could inherit a soldier's belongings. Their sons, too, were normally accepted as Roman citizens if they enrolled in the legion. The marriage ban probably stemmed from official reluctance to pay for army widows' maintenance.

MEDICAL TREATMENT

Although the legionary's life was tough, his medical treatment was remarkably good – in fact, the Roman army's medical care was probably superior to that of any army until the 20th century. As all armies used to lose more men to disease than to

enemy action, this was a major advantage. The care the Romans took with their water supply and drains, seeking out good supplies of fresh water and piping it down to the camps, then carrying the sewage to a spot on a river below any watering place, averted many diseases. They also isolated sick, possibly infectious, soldiers and treated them in special hospitals. At Inchtuthil, the northernmost legionary fortress in Scotland, a special *valetudinarium*, or medical wing, has been revealed with spacious wards and double internal walls, presumably for both thermal and acoustic insulation. Doctors (*medici*) were specially trained and became specialists at operations to remove arrowheads and sling-stones from their legionary patients and at cleaning and binding their wounds. Here the Romans continued the medical traditions of the Greeks, which went back to Hippocrates in the 5th century BC. Roman courage must have been needed on the operating table, as there were no anaesthetics.

Above: These soldiers from the 4th century BC are carrying a dead comrade. From the earliest times, the Romans were willing to accept very high casualties in their wars.

Below: The worship of Mithras, the saviour-god of Persian origin, became very popular in the Roman army.

AUXILIARY TROOPS

Above: The auxiliaries, often drawn from such conquered peoples as shown here in this Hellenistic sculpture, provided much of the cavalry used by the Romans. They did not have stirrups and, although they had spears, fought more with long swords.

Legionaries, the army's backbone, were solely heavy infantry. Intended to fight major battles, they were originally recruited exclusively from Roman citizens. During the Republic, legionaries were supplemented by equal numbers of soldiers from the Latin and Italian allies: the auxiliaries. These supplied lighter troops, including much-needed cavalry. With the extension of the full franchise to the allies in 90BC, they no longer provided such troops, seeking the more prestigious and lucrative posts in the legions. However, auxiliaries became increasingly important as Rome began to defend, as opposed to simply expand, its empire. From Augustus' reign onwards, auxiliaries were systematically recruited from non-Roman citizens. One of their big advantages to the government was that their pay was considerably less (an auxiliary infantryman was paid about half a legionary's rate).

Numidian (North African) cavalry, used to rout Hannibal at the Battle of Zama in 202BC, and other non-Italian auxiliary cavalry, were commonly employed by the mid-2nd century BC. Caesar had made use of the Gallic and German horsemen he encountered in Gaul to help defeat Pompey. But these remained exceptions. In the war between Antony and Augustus in 31BC, their huge forces were still overwhelmingly made up of legionaries. Reducing the army to only 28 legions, or about 150,000 men, and establishing permanent frontiers, Augustus began to employ auxiliaries, chiefly as frontier and policing troops.

The Romans employed auxiliaries as specialists to supplement their heavy infantry: Cretan or Syrian archers, slingers from the Balearics and Numidian, Gallic and later Sarmatian cavalry, 3,800 of whom were sent to Britain to repel an invasion. Auxiliaries can clearly be seen on Trajan's Column, which displays the army of the Principate at its peak in the early 2nd century AD. But most auxiliaries were not specialized forces. By Trajan's time they consisted predominantly of infantry equipped, like the legionaries, with mail shirt, cross-braced helmet, sword and javelins. The major difference was that their arms and armour were cheaper and of lesser quality. Reviewing the Sixth Mounted Cohort of Commagenes in Africa, Hadrian commented dismissively that their appearance and the condition of their weapons matched their (low) level of pay, but he added that they compensated for their scruffiness by their enthusiasm in military exercises. There was a major exception to the inferiority of auxiliaries in Rome's increasing use of cavalry, especially mounted archers, from eastern cities like Palmyra. Many of these auxiliaries started off as levies supplied by client kings on Rome's eastern frontier. They became more important as

Below: Specialized auxiliary troops such as these archers played an increasingly important role in the Roman army from the 1st century AD onwards. In the east, the Romans often used horse archers from Palmyra.

the eastern frontier itself became a problem in the 3rd century AD, and by then were paid more than, in some cases much more than, legionaries.

MANNING THE FRONTIERS

Auxiliaries were organized into smaller units than legions. The infantry was grouped into cohorts of 500 or 1,000 men and cavalry into similarly sized *alae* (literally, wings). These smaller sizes made it easier to move them around, although many resented being transferred, and at first auxiliary cohorts were stationed near their land of origin. A cohort of raw recruits from the Lower Rhine, whom Agricola had stationed in south-west Scotland, revolted at being displaced, murdering their officers and then sailing back to Germany. Shipwrecked and captured by pirates, they ended up as slaves back on the Rhineland. Some auxiliaries recruited from Britain served outside the island, presumably to ensure their loyalty. Auxiliary cohorts became ethnically mixed, with recruits from different areas, although they kept their original names.

The organization, discipline and training of auxiliaries mirrored that of the legions, although the command structure was simpler. Centurions were recruited from the ranks and spent their lives with the same unit. These cohorts were commanded by equestrian tribunes starting off their military careers, or else by decurions from the local aristocracy. The commander of an *ala* of cavalry was a *praefectus alae*, quite a senior post. Mixed cohorts, *cohortes equitatae*, containing about 80 per cent infantry and 20 per cent cavalry, were well suited to the low-intensity policing duties that mostly occupied them. Hadrian's Wall, typical of a fortified frontier, was manned entirely by auxiliaries. There were about 12–15,000 of them housed in forts ranging from tiny towers to big 1,000-men cohort camps such as Housesteads.

Military orders were always given in Latin and sacrifices to the emperor were

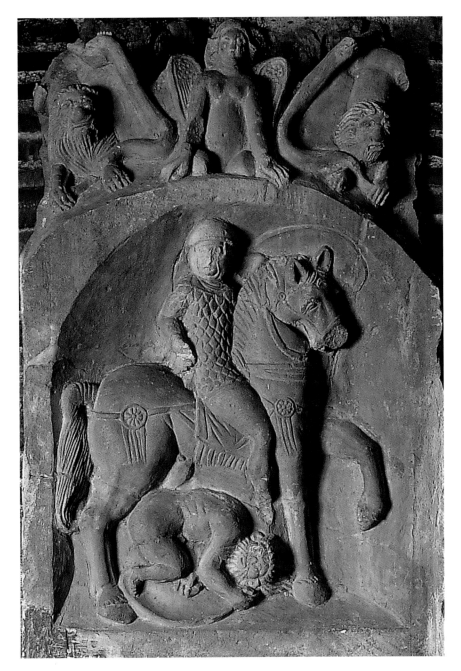

compulsory (hence overtly practising Christians were at first uncommon in the army). After completing 26 years of military service, auxiliaries were rewarded with full Roman citizenship, recorded on a bronze tablet called a *diploma*, and this was a status that their sons inherited. Occasionally an entire cohort received Roman citizenship for outstanding services. Auxiliaries helped spread the Roman way of life. After Caracalla's grant of nearly universal citizenship in AD212, the distinction between auxiliaries and legionaries soon grew blurred.

Above: Memorial to Longinus, a Roman cavalryman of the 1st cohort of Thracians, who died in AD49, aged 40 after 15 years service, and is buried at Colchester. Longinus came from Sardica (modern Sofia) and served a long way from home. The tombstone was found in 1928, but the face was only discovered in 1996.

PITCHING CAMP

Above: Stout stakes with sharpened points lined the palisades of the more heavily fortified camps.

Roman discipline and methodical planning were epitomized by the way that every evening, after marching all day, Roman soldiers constructed elaborate marching camps, always on a rectilinear plan, often for only one night. (These camps left few traces.) Such effort in all conditions required exceptional organization and discipline. Pyrrhus of Epirus realized how formidable his foes were after watching the Romans pitch these camps in 280BC. A century later, Polybius was equally impressed. Such was Roman conservatism that the practice continued throughout the Principate.

One of the best descriptions of the marching camp appears in Pseudo-Hyginus, written in the late 2nd century AD. Every afternoon, towards the end of the day's march, a tribune with centurions would scout ahead to choose the location for that night's camp, ideally a rectangle about 800 yd (731m) long of raised land, clear of trees and with running water nearby. They marked the *praetorium* (the commander's tent) and *principia* (headquarters) with a white flag and then planned the rest of the camp from this centre, using a *groma*, a surveying instrument. The two main streets, the *via principalis* and the *via praetoria*, running through the middle of the camp, were 60ft (18m) wide, lesser ones 50ft (15m) wide. With these streets defined, the lines of the ditch and rampart would be established by spears stuck into the earth at intervals.

Every legionary carried two to three *pila muralia*, palisade stakes about 7ft (2m) long with sharpened points. After they had dug their *fossa* – a trench normally about 3ft (1m) deep and 5ft (1.5m) wide (but deeper and wider if under immediate threat), they planted their stakes in the *agger*, the low rampart formed by the excavated earth, intertwining them so any intruders could

Right: A ditch, rampart and palisade separated the camp from the world outside. A similar arrangement was also used for some frontier installations, here, in a reconstruction of a section of the German frontier, with a watchtower.

not easily remove them. The camp's ramparts, although hard to penetrate and impossible for a unit in formation, did not form defensible barriers but marked it out from its surroundings. Just inside lay the *intervallum*, the space at least 100ft (30m) wide always left empty, to enable the legionaries to deploy within the camp and to bar enemy missiles reaching the tents. All camps were laid out in exactly the same pattern wherever they were. Legionaries camped on either side of the *via praetoria*, the cavalry facing the *via praetoria*, the other auxiliaries and non-Romans being put with the baggage train and cooking tents beyond the *via principalis*. Only the four entrances were more heavily fortified. The legionaries marched out of their allotted gates already armed and in formation.

The *contubernium*, the basic legionary tent, slept eight men. Made of leather, with front and back access, these tents could be rolled up into a sausage shape and carried by mules or ponies. Larger, more elaborate tents were provided for centurions and other officers. That of the general was large enough for administrative and military offices.

Keeping watch was vital. Every evening a guard from the *maniple* or century chosen for the first watch was taken to the tribune's tent and given a *tessera*, a small marked tablet. He surrendered this to a cavalry trooper who made his rounds at fixed hours, collecting the *tesserae* from each guard. If the sentry was absent or asleep, the trooper got witnesses to this. At dawn they reported to the tribune, who checked the *tesserae*. If one sentry had not returned his *tessera*, then he would be tried and cudgelled to death by his comrades, whose lives he had endangered by his inattention. As Polybius dryly commented, "the Roman army's night watches are most punctiliously kept".

Such repeated entrenchments might seem laborious, even wasteful, but they gave the Romans many advantages. By shutting out the possibly alien world and creating a model of Roman order, it helped give soldiers a good night's sleep, protected from surprise night attacks, and left them fresh to face the enemy next day. It also reduced the risk of disease through the properly dug latrines and, not least, impressed possibly hostile observers.

Above: Excavations at Caerleon, the legionary fortress in South Wales, have revealed the network of latrines and waterways at the barracks, a testimony to Roman concerns to keep their army healthy and fighting fit.

ROADS, CANALS AND BRIDGES

Above: The Romans built to last, as this still-surviving, if battered, road across the moors in northern Britain reveals.

Below: The 2nd-century AD road in Petra, the trading city in Jordan. Many roads survive intact in desert areas.

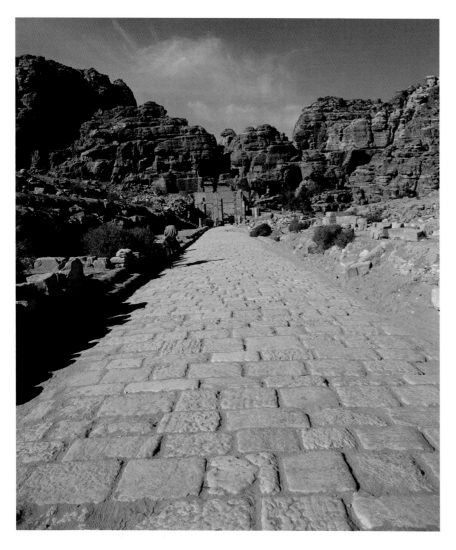

The Roman network of roads was both practical and impressive. The empire was united by 53,000 miles (85,000km) of roads from Scotland to Syria. Often built by legionaries, the roads were designed for troop movements, but civilians soon followed. Under many roads across Europe today lie Roman roads. It was not until the 19th century that Europe saw such a comprehensive road system.

The Greeks had built short stretches of paved roads and in the first Persian empire (*c.*539–331BC) the Royal Road linked the Aegean provinces to the capital Susa, 1,500 miles (2,400km) distant. But none approached the audacious scale of Rome's roads. The first road was the Via Appia, dubbed "Queen of Roads", built in 312BC by Claudius Appius the Censor. Running at first 164 miles (264km) from Rome to Capua to supply armies fighting the Samnites, it was later extended to Brindisi, another 234 miles (377km). It had the hallmarks of a classic Roman road: running as straight as practically possible, it crossed marshes on stone bridges and had a gravel top-dressing (replaced in 295BC by paved stones), good foundations and a proper camber to let water drain away, making it usable in all weathers. It was followed by many others, such as the Via Flaminia in 220BC, running across the Apennines to Rimini. Some roads had overt military intentions. The Via Aemilia, built in 189BC and running unblinkingly straight for 150 miles (240km) from Rimini to Piacenza through northern Italy, was intended to overawe Gallic natives and reassure Roman settlers. It did both. Rome's imperialist road-building did not stop with Italy. In 130BC the Via Egnatia was constructed across the top of Greece from Durazzo to Thessalonica and on to Byzantium (Istanbul). It remained a great imperial highway for 1,200 years.

All roads in the Republic, which helped unite and Romanize a very disparate Italy, were built by *publicani*, contractors working to orders from the state, who would inspect the roads on completion. (The same term applied to tax-farmers.) Under Augustus, the road-building programme became more systematic and ever more impressive. He restored many of Italy's roads and built new ones, some high across Alpine passes such as the St Bernard and Mt Genèvre passes, whose bridge and viaducts still impress travellers. In Gaul, important cities such as Lyons became hubs for a network of roads across the province – north to the Channel, north-east to the Rhine, south to Provence. London became the hub of a similar, if smaller, network, as did Antioch in Syria.

Left: The Roman bridge of Alcantara over the river Tagus in western Spain was built in the early 2nd century AD by Caius Julius Lacer for eleven local towns. It still stands and carries traffic today, which must make it one of the world's oldest functioning bridges.

Along the indeterminate desert frontiers of Arabia Petraea (Jordan), a road built under Trajan acted as a *limes*, a guarded frontier patrolled by cavalry. A similar pattern of patrol roads as *limes* can be seen both in North Africa and in Germany. Along the pan-imperial highways galloped the emperor's emissaries. They changed horses at the imperial posting stations, where they were also fed at the local population's expense. All roads were similarly maintained by corvées of forced labour until the end of the empire. Ironically, Rome's invaders benefited from its excellent paved roads.

CANALS AND BRIDGES

Even for Romans, it was always cheaper to move goods by water than by land. The Mediterranean, with its obligingly many inlets, combined with large rivers – the Rhône, Rhine, Danube, Nile, Tagus – provided a network of waterways. The Rhine and Danube were great military routes with fleets patrolling. The Danube fleet was divided in two, one flotilla operating downriver from the Iron Gates. Rivers were sometimes supplemented by short canals, although there was no canal-building programme. Caesar, like Nero, talked of digging a canal through the rocky mass of the Corinth isthmus, but this vision taxed Roman technology. Traces of Nero's attempt were found when the Corinth Canal was dug in the late 19th century. His builders had stopped when they hit bedrock.

Bridges were not beyond Roman technology and carried Rome's roads across gorges and rivers so successfully that some still stand. The great bridge over the Tagus at Alcantara in Spain was built by the combined efforts of eleven Lusitanian towns in Trajan's reign. Its builder, Caius Julius Lacer, proclaimed in an inscription that his bridge would last forever. In contrast, Caesar threw a timber bridge across the Rhine, then destroyed it, a feat meant to impress Roman audiences as much as Germans. But the most impressive Roman bridge was that built across the Danube at Drobeta by the architect Apollodorus for Trajan's Dacian campaign. With 20 massive stone piers, each 160ft (49m) high, driven into the fast-flowing river over 1000 yds (1000m) wide, and a timber superstructure, it was seen as one of the wonders of the world. Hadrian pulled it down on becoming emperor for reasons of prudence – he said barbarians might cross by it – or through jealousy of Trajan.

Above: Roman soldiers under Trajan (AD98–117) built a remarkable bridge across the Danube, pulled down soon after by Hadrian, and a supporting road along the Iron Gorge's steep cliffs.

FLEETS AND SHIPS

The Mediterranean, which the Romans called both *Mare Internum*, the inner sea, and *Mare Nostrum*, our sea, might appear to be at the centre of the Roman empire. In fact, however, the Romans were never great sailors. Unlike the Greeks, they only turned to controlling the seas when they were forced to. Rome's navy was always markedly inferior in status to its army and the might of the empire was built on land. But in order to conquer and then control their expanding empire, the Romans needed to gain sufficient mastery at sea, having, at the very least, modest permanent fleets – a fact Augustus finally accepted.

Like the other Mediterranean naval powers, the Roman navy consisted of galleys, which were rowed by poorer citizens or allies and very seldom by slaves. By the 3rd century BC these galleys were quinqueremes, with five rows of oars, or triremes, with three rows, arranged in a pattern that is still not entirely clear. Before the development of proper cannon in the 16th century, naval warfare – chiefly ramming and boarding – made galleys the only effective warships in the landlocked waters. However, their large crews of about 300 oarsmen, together with the lack of living space on board, meant that they normally had to be beached at night. Fleets therefore hugged the coasts whenever they could.

The Romans had no navy until their wars against Carthage began in 264BC. As Carthage ruled the western Mediterranean with an efficient navy of galleys mass-produced in its superb double harbours, Rome realized it must build a fleet of its own to fight it. According to Polybius, the Romans modelled their galleys on a stranded Carthaginian ship, quickly building 100 quinqueremes and meanwhile training their oarsmen on tiered benches on land. But their inexperience led initially to defeat, even in harbour. Accepting that they could not match Punic seamanship,

the Romans ingeniously devised the *corvus*, the raven, a boarding ramp fitted with a heavy spike which swivelled on a pole set on the ship's prow. This ramp, about 40ft (12m) long and 4ft (1.2m) wide, was swung over the deck of the enemy ship and dropped on to it, locking the two galleys together. Roman marines – 120 of them to a galley – then swarmed across to overwhelm the Carthaginians.

This tactic won several victories over the startled Carthaginians, beginning with Mylae in 260BC and continuing at Ecnomus in 256BC, where each side mustered over 300 ships according to Polybius. The Romans then grew over-confident, sending huge invasion fleets to Africa to support Regulus' invasion, most of which were sunk in storms. The *corvus* may have made the galleys – always fragile vessels – top-heavy, and the Romans never used it again after finally defeating the Carthaginians in 241BC.

Under the terms of the subsequent treaty Carthage gave up most of her navy, and during the Second Punic War (218–201BC) her ships tried to avoid the now indisputably superior Romans, as did the Macedonian ships. Philip V's 100-strong fleet sailed into the Adriatic in 216BC but fled at the sight of only ten Roman quinqueremes. From the mid-2nd century BC the Romans let their fleet decay, as there seemed to be no naval rivals left. They relied instead on Greek ships to transport their troops, failing to realize the importance of the Rhodian fleet in maintaining freedom of the sea. Rhodes' navy declined after the opening of Delos as a free port in 168BC, and pirates took advantage of this, raiding right up to Ostia and capturing two praetors in 68BC. Pompey was appointed emergency commander under the *Lex Gabinia* to quash them, with a fleet of 200 galleys, which were mostly supplied by Greek cities. With this fleet he swept the seas clean, but in the subsequent civil wars

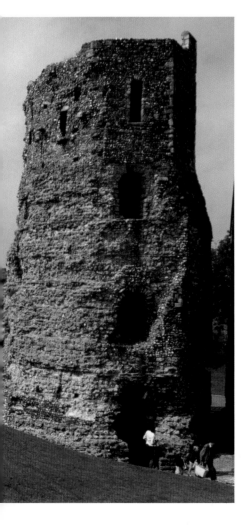

Below: This Roman pharos *(lighthouse) lies within the ruins of medieval Dover Castle in England. It was one of numerous lighthouses built along the coasts of the empire.*

(49–30BC) fleets multiplied. Sextus Pompeius had a large fleet with which he cut Rome's grain supply until defeated with the aid of Antony's ships at Naulochus in 36BC. The final battle in the civil wars was the naval contest at Actium, in which Antony and Cleopatra's Roman-Egyptian fleet was cornered and defeated by Agrippa, Octavian's general, who traditionally used smaller Liburnian galleys against Antony's quinqueremes.

THE IMPERIAL NAVY

Augustus disbanded most of the huge fleets that victory brought him – some 700 ships – but, needing to safeguard Rome's grain imports, he did not close down the navy. Instead, he set up three small fleets at Misenum in the Bay of Naples, at Ravenna and at Fréjus, using the mainly Greek ships and crews he already had as their core. The fleet at Fréjus shrank to a mere flotilla. There were also river fleets on the Rhine, Danube and Nile and a small fleet on the Black Sea. Later a fleet, the *classis britannica*, was created to patrol the English Channel and southern North Sea. From the mid-3rd century AD this British fleet was used chiefly against the Saxon pirates who were becoming increasingly common. Commanded by prefects under imperial orders, the navy offered a similar career to the army's auxiliaries. After 26 years, sailors received Roman citizenship at the end of their service.

Ships were commanded by *trierarchs*, squadrons by *navarchs*, both names indicating the Greek origins of the fleet.

For a long period, the whole of the Mediterranean was kept peaceful by these measures, essential for the empire's well-being. If it was sometimes swifter to move troops by sea than by land, it was almost always cheaper to transport goods by ship. The 3rd-century AD crisis revealed that these fleets had become inadequate, however, as Goths and other barbarians seized shipping and turned pirate, and they were expanded. Later, the Byzantine empire relied heavily on its navy, but the Byzantine empire was predominantly Greek, and the Greeks always retained a strong maritime tradition.

Above: Navies in the ancient world consisted of galleys such as these biremes. They had huge crews of up to 300 oarsmen (not usually slaves in either Greece or Rome), essential to propel the ships to ram and board opponents.

Below: The main port of Rome at Portus, north of Ostia, with the artificial harbours built by Claudius (right) and Trajan (left) to help the import of grain. The canal linked the port with the Tiber, while the pharos guided shipping into port.

CHAPTER III

ARMS AND THE MEN

The Roman army was one of the most effective fighting forces in history, but its weapons were not normally superior to those of its enemies. Most Roman weaponry was simple: a short sword, a javelin, a coat of mail or armour plates, greaves (leg armour), and a rectangular or oval shield. Against often more numerous northern barbarians, the Romans did have some technical advantages: their armour was better, their catapults alarmingly formidable. All these, however, were secondary to Roman discipline and courage. How the Romans used their weapons was what counted; and it was their *virtus*, their courage and ability, that Romans celebrated, not their technological prowess. When necessary, they made other people's weapons, be they catapults, slings or armour, part of their own standard equipment. This Roman adaptability, coupled with ruthless determination and refusal to surrender, were Rome's real secret weapons.

In only two spheres were the Romans true innovators: the maniple and the cohort, tactical formations within the legion that helped them beat Hannibal and the Greeks, and the massive fortifications of the later empire. These constituted the most formidable walls yet seen anywhere in the world. Their effectiveness is shown by the thousand-year survival of Constantinople, whose walls enabled the new Rome to live on when the old Rome fell.

Left: The Romans made good use of catapults and other artillery in siege warfare. Encircling siege walls was also frequently used to prevent movement from the besieged town or camp.

ARMOUR

*Above: The higher grades of cavalry (*alae*) wore elaborate helmets to mark their rank. This is a 3rd-century AD cavalry helmet.*

Below: The long, curved shield was standard issue for legionaries in the Principate from the 1st century AD.

Roman armour in the early Republic (5th century BC) was influenced by Rome's neighbours, the Etruscans, who in turn emulated the Greeks. Etruscans adopted the Greek hoplite method of fighting – heavily armoured spearmen grouped in *phalanxes* – and their armour reflected this. It consisted of greaves (shin armour), a bronze cuirass (breastplate) and a helmet with long cheek guards and high crests. However, as the Romans evolved their own uniquely flexible system of *maniples* and legions after 400BC, they began to develop their own lighter armour, which varied according to the wealth of the Roman concerned, for at that time and for long after, each soldier armed and armoured himself.

The first two lines of heavy infantry in each *maniple* – the *hastati* and *principes* – wore a modest-sized square breastplate called a *pectorale* (breast guard) and one greave for the left leg, the one that was thrust out when fighting. Wealthier legionaries, especially those of the *triarii*, sometimes wore mail shirts, but these could be very heavy, weighing over 30lb (14kg). After the Roman defeat at Lake Trasimene in 218BC, some soldiers who tried to escape by swimming were drowned by the weight of their armour. The legionaries all wore bronze Montefortino-type helmets (named after the place where some were found). These had two tall, feathered plumes 2ft (60cm) high sticking out of them to make the soldiers look taller, long cheek guards and a double chin strap. For defence, the legionaries depended on their long, semi-cylindrical body shields. These were about 4ft (1.2m) long and about 2ft (60cm) wide. Reconstructions show that these shields weighed at least 22lb (10kg). They were made of two sheets of wood glued together, covered with canvas and calf skin. The shields could also be used as weapons to knock the enemy over. The *veles*, light infantry

recruited from the poorer citizens, had no armour and so they wore animal skins over their helmets to help their officers recognize them.

From the time of the late Republic (100BC), after Marius' reforms, legionaries were far more uniformly equipped and armoured. The ordinary legionaries wore long mail coats and Montefortino-style helmets, but with horsehair plumes that hung down, and carried long oval shields very similar to the earlier shields. Officers (centurions and tribunes) often wore "muscled" – modelled to the body – cuirasses with greaves over leather tunics, ribbons of rank around their waists – a Greek idea – and elaborate Italo-Corinthian helmets. Some of the armour of this period was of poor quality, probably reflecting the massive demands made on armourers by the fast-growing armies of the civil wars.

By the early 1st century AD, with the Principate firmly established, workshops were set up to mass-produce the body armour the legionaries needed. The standard helmet evolved from the jockey type, which recalled a reversed jockey's cap in the late Republic, to the "Imperial Gallic helmet". Partly inspired by Gallic examples, the latter had an enlarged neck guard and long cheek guards, with a reinforcing strip across the front of the cap to protect the face from a downward cut. With added ear guards, this became the standard Roman infantry helmet over the next two centuries. It was usually made of iron, which was always cheaper than bronze, if less durable. Such a helmet gave a high degree of protection while allowing soldiers to hear and see clearly.

Equally flexible and protective was the *lorica segmentata*, the name given to a type of banded armour developed in the 1st century AD, the first full example of which was excavated at Corbridge. This had bands of soft untempered iron plates forming a corselet, or cuirass, which was buckled on. Such armour was brilliant at

ARMOURED HORSEMEN

Cavalry in the Principate came in many forms. Light Numidian horsemen had no armour or saddles, but, at the other extreme, some cavalry would qualify as "heavy" by most standards. Although these heavy horsemen did not have stirrups, they had saddles with four pommels (two of which were at the back corners), which gave them some support when mounted. They wore helmets that covered their ears, with extended cheek and neck guards to protect against sword slashes – lances were generally seldom used. Some wore *lorica hamata*, mail coats, some modest-scale armour weighing perhaps 20lb (9kg). The higher grades of cavalry (*alae*) had elaborate helmets and shields, but their horses wore no armour at all.

absorbing blows and not too heavy – it weighed about 20lb (9kg). This made it lighter than the cheaper, more easily maintained, main alternative, the *lorica hamata*, a mail coat worn by some legionaries and by the auxiliary infantry. The *lorica hamata* was heavy, weighing over 30lb (14kg). In the 1st century AD, the oval shield was replaced by a rectangular curved shield, made of three layers of thin strips of wood, encased in leather and covered with a linen layer, its rim reinforced with bronze. The handgrip in its centre was reinforced by an iron or bronze boss. Auxiliaries normally had a simpler version of the Imperial Gallic helmet and a flat oval shield.

ARMOUR IN THE LATER EMPIRE

The types of armour in the later empire reflect the increasing divergence between the mobile *comitatenses* and elite *Palatini* – and the lowly *limitanei* (frontier guard). The Romans encountered real heavy cavalry, the *cataphracti*, around AD100 when Sarmatian riders appeared on the Danube. They were soon employed as auxiliaries, and in the 3rd century AD the Romans began to imitate them. The typical *cataphract* wore mail weighing at least 60lb (27kg), covering him from hooded head to knee; his horse also wore mail armour. An even more heavily armoured cavalryman wore the *lorica squamata*, scale armour, according to graffiti from Dura-Europus. Such armour looked magnificent when well polished, but must have been uncomfortably hot – *clibanarius* means "oven man". The infantry, meanwhile, demoted from their primary battle-fighting role, wore crude iron *intercisa* helmets and relatively little armour. Apparently this was partly a matter of choice – for they now found it too heavy to march or drill in armour – but it made them less effective.

Above: By the 1st century AD, most legionaries wore a type of armour called the lorica segimentata. *This, with banded soft iron plates, was laced at the back and gave excellent protection, but it was expensive.*

ARMS: SWORDS, DAGGERS, BOWS, *PILA* AND SLINGS

Above: Sword and dagger.

The Roman soldiers of the early Republic (509–*c*.350BC) were armed in the prevailing Greco-Etruscan style as hoplites – heavy spearmen with long pikes and swords and small round shields. However, by the 4th century BC the new legions of maniples, the army's smallest fighting units, who were starting to fight in the *quincunx*, or chequerboard pattern, required quite different types of arms.

The basic weapon the Roman legionary now acquired, and which he was to use to create the Roman empire, was the *gladius hispaniensis*, the "Spanish sword". This may have been inspired by Spanish examples, but it was probably being used before Rome had any direct experience of Spain. This sword, which had a blade less than 3ft (1m) long, was wickedly sharp and well suited to both cutting and thrusting. Its long, tapering point of highly tempered steel meant that it could pierce most opponents' armour. Roman swordsmanship was generally much better than that of their adversaries, but the legionaries were also helped by having swords of a quality that only chieftains could afford among most of their enemies.

The *gladius* evolved from the Mainz-type *gladius* to the slightly longer Pompeii type, which could cut as well as thrust. (These swords are named after the places where examples were found.) Roman cavalry, for a long time very secondary in importance, used a longer sword, the *spatha*, which was about 3ft (1m) in length. In the later empire, this longer sword was adopted by most Roman infantrymen, but by then infantry had become very inferior to cavalry. Legionaries wore their swords on their right, probably because their heavy shields on their left would have made it awkward to draw after hurling their other principal weapon. In contrast, centurions, wore their swords on the left, possibly because they carried their shields only some of the time.

Almost equally important to the legionary of Rome's golden age of military might was the *pilum*, the javelin or throwing spear. Each legionary in the first two rows of the earlier legions, the *hastati* and the *principes*, carried two *pila*, which came in two thicknesses according to Polybius. The *pilum* had a thin wooden shaft about 4ft (1.2m) long, with a pyramid-shaped barbed iron head on top of a thin iron neck. When thrown,

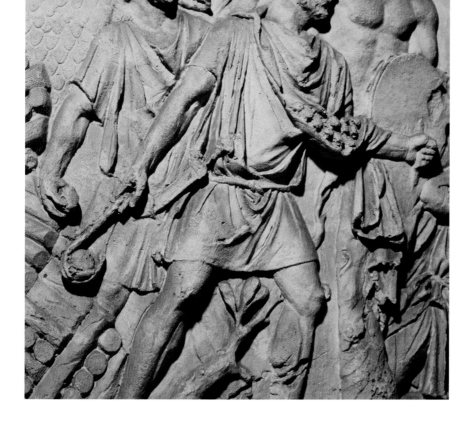

Left: A slinger in the Dacian wars, one of the many auxiliary soldiers.

this could often go right through an enemy's shield, but if it did not, the point would stick in the shield and the neck bend, so making the shield useless. An enemy would then have to throw it away, leaving himself exposed to the merciless cutting thrusts of the legionary. (Marius later revised the *pilum* by making it bend even more effectively. It is possible that he was also responsible for adding the weights halfway down the *pilum*'s shaft.)

A *pilum*'s absolute maximum range was about 100ft (30m), although its effective range was only half that. Roman troops painfully acquired the discipline required to wait until the enemy was that close before discharging a devastating volley. The *triarii* were armed with long spears that could be used as pikes until Marius' reforms, when all legionaries received the same equipment. Although primarily intended for throwing, the *pilum* could also be used as a stationary weapon to repel cavalry, when the first row would kneel, bracing the butts of their *pila* on the ground so that they formed a spiked barrier. Behind them, other rows would launch their *pila* at the cavalry, whose horses would not cross such a seemingly solid barrier. Legionaries also had the *pugio*, a dagger about 8in (20cm) long, which was worn on the left hip, but this seems to have been given up in the Principate. Such simple but devastating weapons, when used in the right hands, made the Roman legionary appear almost invincible.

THE AUXILIARIES' WEAPONS

Auxiliary infantrymen of the Principate used much the same weapons as the legionaries, but the other, more specialized, types of auxiliary obviously had different kinds of weapons. Slingers, traditionally recruited from the Balearic islands, used simple slings, as did the club men, both being skirmishing light troops, but they were not significant parts of the army. However, the archers whom Rome employed, at first from Crete but later from many sources including Syria, were at times vital. They normally had composite bows, made of bone and sinew as well as wood, which fired arrows further than simple wooden bows.

The *alae* (literally, wings) of auxiliary cavalry also gained increasing importance. Although they often charged with spears or lances, their impact was small compared to later cavalry charges owing to their lack of stirrups, for which the "horns" of their saddles only partly compensated. This must have hampered the effectiveness of the heavily armoured *cataphracts*. The stirrup is first mentioned only in the *Strategikon*, a military manual written by the East Roman (Byzantine) emperor Maurice (AD582–602). In the later empire, the *limitanei* carried several *mattiobarbului*, lead-weighted darts, which they kept inside their shields, instead of the *pilum*. These smaller missiles would have been particularly useful when defending forts, which was now the chief duty of *limitanei*.

Above: This detail from the Roman triumphal arch in Orange, southern France, shows hand-to-hand fighting with the gladius.

Below: Roman legionaries used many varieties of sword, all based on the gladius hispaniensis, *or Spanish stabbing sword. These two examples date from the 1st century* AD, *near the zenith of Roman power.*

ARTILLERY

Above: The onager *(wild ass) was a primitive but highly effective catapult, capable of lobbing large weights surprising distances. It was used mostly in sieges and for defending fortresses, being too immobile for battlefield use.*

Below: This complex late Roman catapult, a ballista fulminalis, *could shoot its bolt or spear up to 300yd (275m). While slow, such catapults could be devastating, terrifying barbarians.*

In the earlier Republic, Rome's armies had little in the way of artillery or catapults. In the epic siege of Veii (406–396BC), the formidably well-fortified Etruscan city, for example, they relied chiefly on surprise to capture the city, eventually digging a tunnel under the walls and crawling up an irrigation channel by night. But in their expansion across the Mediterranean after 264BC, the Romans came across the varied catapults developed by the Greeks (especially by Philip II of Macedon) and learnt how to employ such "artillery", the only kind there was before gunpowder.

The Romans' lack of development in such armaments mirrored the general lack of technological progress in civilian life. Compared to medieval Europe, or even to the Greeks, Roman civilization made few technological innovations. Nonetheless, the Romans adopted earlier discoveries, often to good effect. After the disaster at the Battle of Adrianople in AD378, for example, the Goths were dissuaded from further attacks on the walls of Adrianople by a single bolt fired from a Roman scorpion-type catapult.

WEAPONS OF BOMBARDMENT

There were two basic types of artillery, according to Vitruvius, who was writing in the 1st century BC. The first was the catapult type, among which was the typical *catapulta*, a two-armed torsion catapult firing either bolts or stones. Similar was the *scorpio*, a light, bolt-shooting *ballista*. Both operated on the crossbow principle, with a pair of vertical coil chambers at the front; the bow was drawn back by a windlass and held by a rack and pinion. When the bow was released, the bolt shot along a groove and out through an opening in the front in a flat trajectory. These stationary catapults could fire iron bolts up to 300yd (275m) with some accuracy. In AD363 during the Persian campaign, an officer standing next to Julian was killed by a bolt aimed at the emperor. The Persians used much the same weapons as the Romans.

The *carroballista* was a *scorpio* mounted on a mule-drawn cart; it could be used in the field to fire bolts with large heads up to 1ft (30cm) long, which made a formidable arrow. According to Vegetius – who, writing around AD400, may not be completely accurate – each century of the traditional Roman army had a *carroballista*. Used on the flanks of the legion, they fired barrages over the heads of the legionaries.

The other, much heavier, type of catapult was nicknamed the *onager* (wild ass) because of its kick. This was a slower-firing, lower-tension catapult, based on the principles of a sling rather than a crossbow, but one capable of lobbing huge stones at walls or troops. Josephus records that at the Siege of Jerusalem in AD70, the Tenth Legion had machines that could hurl stones weighing a *talent* (55lb/25kg) about 400yd (360m).

Battle stones found at British forts, such as High Rochester, north of Hadrian's Wall, weigh over 100lb (45kg).

THE SECRET WEAPONS THAT ROME IGNORED

As Romans in the 4th century AD knew too well, the empire faced unremitting threats from without and ever-growing manpower shortages within. Although most Roman armies remained better equipped than their barbarian opponents, this did not make up for their lack of numbers. Attempts to cope with the shortage of Roman recruits by recruiting barbarian *foederati* were not only inherently risky but were also leading to the de-Romanization of the army itself. Vegetius, the best-known military writer of the period, advocated a return to the stringent discipline of earlier years, which had underlain Roman triumphs down the centuries, without success.

However, the anonymous writer of *De Rebus Bellicis* (About Wars), who probably lived in the middle of the 4th century AD, had different and more ingenious ideas. He proposed what were in effect a variety of super-weapons with which the Romans might make up for their lack of numbers and their decline in fighting spirit. One such weapon that he proposed was a horse-drawn, arrow-firing catapult that could be swivelled around completely on a four-wheeled cart, and which could be mechanically elevated or lowered to control the trajectory of fire. Another super-weapon he proposed was a mobile armoured shield beneath which attackers could approach a wall – a development of the *testudo*, tortoise formation, of locked shields. He also envisaged a variety of armoured chariots, one with scythed wheels – almost looking back to the scythed chariots once used by Celts and Persians – pulled by armoured horses. At sea, where there was a shortage of oarsmen for the galleys, he cleverly thought of using ox-power to turn a capstan on deck. Through a series of cogs and gears this would have powered two paddle-wheels, one on each side of his novel warship, which he called a *liburna*. Whether or not his schemes, at times anticipating more recent war machines, were at all practical given the technology and resources of the time, nothing came of them.

Only one much later invention really worked: that of *Greek fire*, which was a flame-thrower, using the siphon principles to project a form of liquid fire, highly effective against ships and siege engines. This invention traditionally helped to save Constantinople from Arab attacks at the end of the 7th century AD.

Above: Roman legionaries loading an onager-*type catapult at the siege of Alesia in Gaul in 52BC, one of the epic Roman sieges. These cumbersome stone-throwing catapults were normally only used in sieges, or later for defending fortresses.*

Below: Roman legionaries, played by re-enactors, loading a carroballista-*type catapult. A bolt-firing machine on the same principles as the crossbow, this was mobile enough to be used in battle, but its chief role was for attacking or defending forts.*

Special reinforced platforms were built for firing such machines from within forts in the later empire. Technically, the *onager* was a relatively crude machine: its arm was pulled back, tightening the coiled ropes that propelled it, and a sling at the end of its arm was filled with a stone and then released, with a tremendous kick, to be stopped by a padded beam. According to Vegetius, perhaps overstating ancient strengths, each legion had ten *onagri*, one for each cohort, drawn on carriages by oxen. Used *en masse* they were highly effective in siege warfare, either for offence or defence, but they were too immobile to be of much use on the battlefield, unlike the *carroballista*.

SIEGE WARFARE

Above: This detail from Trajan's Column in Rome shows legionaries assaulting walls during the wars in Dacia, a formidably well-defended kingdom.

Below: Legionaries building double wooden walls to bi-circumvallate Alesia, to prevent Gaulish armies from relieving the besieged inside.

The Romans brought to siege-craft their customary determination and aggression. Our word siege comes from the French *siège*, sitting out. In contrast, the Roman word *oppugnatio* means assault, attacking a city relentlessly. In contrast to elaborate Greek siege machinery, the Romans preferred simpler methods. These included bi-circumvallation, building double walls to stop relief getting in. They were also masters of battering rams.

When the Romans attacked the large Greek city of Agrigento (Acragas) in Sicily in 262BC, they built a line of forts around the city, connected these by walls with watchtowers and starved the city into surrender. If an enemy army was in the field, they built a second wall facing outward. They first used bi-circumvallation besieging Lilybaeum in the First Punic War. The greatest bi-circumvallation was at Alesia in 52BC, where Caesar bottled up Vercingetorix and defied a relief Gaulish army.

At ports such as Lilybaeum in Sicily, where complete enclosure was impossible, the Romans tried to close in the harbour with earth, although at Lilybaeum this was washed away by the sea and they captured the city by assault. Syracuse, changing sides after Hannibal's victory at Cannae, presented Rome with its biggest challenge in scientific siege warfare in 213BC. Marcellus, the Roman commander, controlled the sea, but Syracuse harbour was heavily fortified. The Romans made a simultaneous attack by land and sea, using 50 galleys filled with archers, slingers and javelineers. Eight galleys were tied together in pairs and on each a wide ladder was raised. This was the same height as the walls. But the scientist Archimedes, masterminding Syracusan defences, arranged catapults to fire at fixed ranges so that the Romans faced devastating fire. Marcellus tried a night attack to avoid this, but Archimedes designed huge cranes that swung out from behind the walls and dropped stones on the Roman galleys. Others lowered giant grappling hooks, which pulled the ships up and released them to capsize. Finally the Romans captured Syracuse by stealth. Archimedes was killed in the sack of the city.

Roman tenacity caused many cities to capitulate before the siege started. A story relates how a Roman commander, about to besiege a city, was told by its envoys that they had enough food for ten years. The Roman replied that in that case he would capture the city in the eleventh year. The city surrendered. If it did not surrender, a city faced obliteration. According to the current rules of warfare, once the head of a battering ram touched the enemy's walls or gate, no mercy could be expected and Romans never gave it. From Cartagena in 209BC to Jerusalem in AD70, the Romans systematically killed every living thing in the cities they captured – even dogs – apart from attractive women and children, whom they raped and sold into slavery. Such exemplary terror generally worked. However, Roman commanders preferred to starve a city into submission, because its booty became theirs, whereas in an assault the troops were permitted to sack a city and take what they could.

BATTERING RAMS

The Romans excelled at battering rams, the most basic siege tool. The name comes from its head, a massive iron hammer in the shape of a ram's head. It was fixed to a huge beam in a very strong shed, often on wheels, with a steep-pitched roof covered in hides from animals recently butchered so that their wet skins would repel any fire arrows. Vitruvius and Vegetius describe similar sheds of varying sizes, sometimes called *testudo arietaria*, after the tortoise. This name was also given to formations of men carrying linked shields above their heads. High towers of timber could be rolled forward to protect them by shooting arrows and javelins. If effective against

Mesopotamian mud and Mediterranean stone walls, metal rams were of little use against the timber and turf ramparts of north Europe. Caesar describes a *murus Gallicus* (Gallic wall), stone-faced but its centre filled with soil. Laced with timbers, it was impervious to normal rams. Usually other forms of assault had to be found.

The other great siege tactic was mining a wall. A mine would be dug under a city wall, supported by wooden props that, when ignited, caused the tunnel and the wall above it to collapse. As defenders could hear the tunnellers, they often made counter-mines, causing the attackers' tunnel to collapse. The besieged also mined under the bulky towers of the attackers, causing them to keel over. On the eastern front, especially when the Sassanids replaced the Parthians, there were long and elaborate sieges, as at Dura-Europus in c.AD256 and at Amida in AD359. In both cases, these fortified Roman cities fell to the Persians only after long, expensive sieges.

Above: A Renaissance view of a triumph of Julius Caesar shows the spoils and varied war engines used in his conquest of Gaul, including the siege of Alesia in 52BC.

Below: A medieval drawing of a Roman four-wheeled horse-drawn carroballista, *the mobile type of catapult used in battle as well as siege warfare.*

TRIUMPHS AND OVATIONS

On returning to Rome after defeating a (foreign) enemy, a general of the Republic could expect to be awarded the highest accolade, a triumph. According to legend, this celebration dated back to the birth of Rome and Romulus' defeat of Acron, king of the Ceninenses. Wearing a laurel wreath, Romulus led his men singing in triumphant procession to thank Jupiter. The ceremony was influenced by the Etruscans, who added a chariot and other details, including the ceremonial clothes and red-painted face of the *triumphator*, the triumphant general. As the empire grew, the ceremony also grew in splendour. It continued far into the Principate, but by then only members of the imperial family received a full triumph.

The *triumphator* was clad in the *toga picta*, a purple toga edged with gold, over a purple tunic and gilded shoes. He carried an ivory sceptre topped by an eagle, the bird of Jupiter, and an olive branch while wearing a laurel wreath, on his solemn procession to Jupiter's temple to give thanks for his victory. The procession started in the Campus Martius (field of Mars) just outside the *pomerium*, the sacred boundary. At its head were magistrates and senators; next came the horn-blowers, heading a long train of bearers laden with booty. They were followed by models or paintings of captured cities or battles won. Next came priests leading the white sacrificial oxen with gilded horns, with children carrying the *paterae*, golden saucers to catch the oxen's blood. Then came the captives in chains. The *triumphator* brought up the rear in a horse-drawn chariot, with his children beside him and surrounded by crowds of *ludiones*, Etruscan-style dancers. To balance all this, a slave standing behind the *triumphator* whispered in his ear, "Remember, you are mortal." Behind the general came any citizens whom he had

Below: Caesar's final triumph, as depicted in this Renaissance painting. His many victories were celebrated with unparalleled magnificence and splendour.

TRIUMPHAL ARCHES
Among the most distinctive features of the Roman empire were the triumphal arches built to proclaim its victories. The most famous arches are in Rome itself. The Arch of Titus, dedicated in AD81, is among the best preserved; it graphically commemorates Titus' capture of Jerusalem in AD70, and shows the seven-branched candlestick taken from the Temple. Arches, of which many survive, were erected right across the empire, from Jordan to Britain. A vast arch almost 100ft (30m) high and square was erected at Richborough, the chief port of entry to Britain, probably during the AD90s to celebrate Emperor Domitian's supposed conquest of the north of the island. Cased in Cararra marble with gilded bronze statues, it did not long survive Domitian's assassination in AD96.

Above: This Arch of Trajan dominates the ruins of the colony for veterans the emperor founded at Timgad in Africa.

In the Principate, triumphs were reserved for the emperor, and generals had to be content with an *ovatio*, an ovation, in which they sacrificed on the Alban hill and entered Rome on a horse the next day. With this came the grant of *insignia triumphalia*, triumphal ornaments, the right to wear triumphal uniform and a laurel wreath at official ceremonies and have a statue among former triumphators. From Trajan's reign on, all consuls seem to have had the right to such triumphal dress, which must soon have devalued it.

Below: Wearing a special painted toga and clutching a golden sceptre, the triumphant general Scipio Africanus, who had beaten Hannibal, is escorted through the streets of Rome to the Capitoline Hill, where captives were traditionally sacrificed.

freed from captivity, and last of all his victorious soldiers, wearing olive wreaths and singing verses that alternately honoured and mocked their general.

The procession entered by the Forum Boarium (cattle market) and wound through the Circus Maximus, round the Palatine Hill and up the Sacred Way to the Forum, before ascending the Capitoline Hill. Here the leading captives were taken away and sacrificed with the oxen. However, after Aemilius Paullus' triumph in 167 BC, they were normally spared if they had fought bravely. Only those who had broken their word to Rome, like Jugurtha the Numidian king and Vercingetorix the Gallic leader, were executed. Caratacus, the British prince, and Zenobia, Queen of Palmyra, were both spared to live in comfortable obscurity. Cleopatra, however, chose suicide over such ignominy.

Under the Republic, triumphs became more splendid, each successful general proclaiming his – and his family's – glory ever more grandly, despite the efforts of senators to curtail it. Their monuments, statues and, from the mid-3rd century BC, temples all along the triumphal route formed a permanent memorial to their achievements, beautifying the city.

PERMANENT FORTIFICATIONS

Above: Reconstruction of a tower and the walls of the legionary camp at Xanten on the Rhine in Germany. This was originally a two-legion camp. The tower, like most built in the Principate, has a wide gate and was not designed for prolonged defence.

By AD150 Rome had surrounded its empire with permanent defences in stone, wood and turf, some still impressive today. But these walls and ramparts were not intended as impregnable defences. Instead, they were built as bases from which troops would march out to fight. Even the grandest wall, Hadrian's Wall across northern England, was intended not as an impermeable barrier but to control movements across the frontier.

The Servian Wall around Rome built in the 370s BC was massive – 10ft (3m) wide and 30ft (9m) high – enough to defy even Hannibal. But after this war, Rome no longer needed such domestic defences, as its frontiers became ever more distant. When the Rhine and Danube became Rome's *de facto* northern Continental frontiers after Augustus, Roman camps along them developed into permanent stone-built fortresses.

These fortresses were generally built on flat ground for convenience, rather than for defence. Each followed a rectilinear plan derived from marching camps. The fortress of the Sixteenth Legion at Neuss on the Lower Rhine is typical: a rectangle 500 by 700yd (450 by 650m) with walls 15ft (4.5m) high and a surrounding ditch. The walls were intended to protect only against surprise attacks. The *principia*, or legionary head-quarters, where legionary records and standards were kept, faced the legate's house, the *praetorium*, an imposing edifice built around a courtyard, often with hypocaust underfloor heating in northern Europe. Barrack blocks, where the legionaries slept eight to a room, lined the perimeter, with a large gap between them and the walls to allow troops to form up. With workshops, baths, granaries and a hospital, the legionary camp was almost self-sufficient. The auxiliaries' cohorts had similar, if smaller, forts.

Although still committed to taking the offensive, the Romans came to build extensive lines to control their frontiers. The gap between the upper Rhine and the Danube was covered by the advance under the Flavians and Trajan to a line along the Taunus Mountains and River Neckar, then south-east to the Danube near Regensburg. Shortening the frontier, this was defended not by a stone wall but by timber, later stone, towers. These were connected by *limes*, patrolled frontiers,

Right: Another view of the partially reconstructed tower and walls at Xanten on the Rhine. This shows how towers under the Principate did not protrude and how the walls did not have deep moats in front, being designed merely to break the impact of attack.

Right: The ruins of Aquinicum, a legionary fortress near Budapest on the Danube, overlooked by a modern white building.

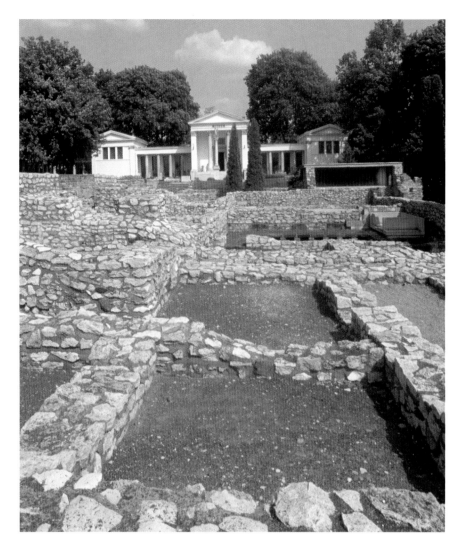

defined as much as defended by a narrow wooden palisade, with forts for auxiliary cohorts every few miles. There were almost 100 camps, connected by 1,500 towers, along this new 310-mile (500km) frontier. They signalled to each other using heliographs (sun signals), smoke or fires. Guarding the Rhine from Bonn to the North Sea, forts lined the west bank, with watchtowers between. A similar chain ran down the Danube to the Black Sea, the river serving instead of a palisade.

In North Africa, where the threat came from fast-moving Berber raiders, the long desert frontier was defended by other *limes*. Low, continuous walls, and a series of *fossata*, deep, flat-bottomed ditches or trenches, formed unmanned but continuous barriers inland from the wheat and olive lands of Rome's bread-basket. Although raiding Berbers could cross walls by breaking them down, they were slowed down and forced to return laden with booty through the same gap. There, waiting Roman patrols from nearby forts could cut them off. These barriers made it difficult for the Berbers to raid at will. Such crossing places corresponded to recognized transhumance routes (used by seasonally migrating flocks of sheep) and provided patrolled crossing points to collect customs dues.

HADRIAN'S WALL

The most imposing and monumental of Roman fortifications is Hadrian's Wall. Hadrian ordered its construction during his visit to Britain in AD122, although his original plan was not fully implemented. Running 76 miles (120km) between the Tyne and Solway, the wall was first built partly in turf and timber, only the eastern 45 miles (73km) being built of stone from the beginning. The wall was about 18ft (5.5m) high and 6–8ft (1.9–2.4m) wide, with a ditch that was about 25ft (7.6m) wide and about 10ft (3m) deep,

with another ditch, the *vallum*, behind. This second ditch was to keep civilians out of the military zone and to channel traffic to customs points. Every Roman mile there was a milecastle, with gates opening to the north flank and two turrets between. These were usually tiny – about 14sq ft (1.3sq m) inside – but the milecastles had garrisons of a century. About 15,000 auxiliaries were deployed along or around the wall. Most were not strung out along it but concentrated in camps for 500 or 1,000 men, such as Housesteads, from which they issued forth to deal with intruders. The wall was not a hermetic frontier but controlled traffic and impressed natives. Forts like High Rochester, 30 miles (48km) north, provided advance posts, while strong reinforcements could be summoned from the legionary fortress at York to the south.

Below: The fort at Vindolanda (Bardon Mill) lies south of Hadrian's Wall in Northumberland, with part of the actual wall reconstructed.

THE GREAT FORTS
OF THE LATER EMPIRE

Above: Sited on the right (hostile) bank of the Rhine, the massive fortress of Deutz was built by Constantine I in AD310. Huge circular towers and walls 65ft (20m) high were designed to overawe the barbarians as well as repel their actual attacks.

Below: Pevensey Castle on the south coast of England was one of a string of the massive fortresses on what became known as the Saxon Shore, built to provide secure bases for the fleets patrolling against invading Saxon pirates.

Changes in the Roman army in the later 3rd and early 4th century AD turned it from a fundamentally offensive force to a predominantly defensive one. They also changed its approach to fortification. The Romans finally began to build fortresses that, with their huge towers and complex gatehouses, looked like real castles, rather than barracks surrounded by quite thin walls. Like real castles also, these forts came to control important passes and crossings and were built on easily defended sites. From the mid-4th century AD, they also grew increasingly cramped inside, in stark contrast to the spacious bases of the Principate. Such castles, cripplingly expensive to build, anticipate those of the Middle Ages.

In the AD260s, Gallienus had begun to reorganize the army and Aurelian had given Rome its new wall in AD272–5, but it was only under Diocletian (AD284–305) that the radical shift to a new type of fort-building fully emerged. It can be seen right across the empire – even in parts not controlled by Diocletian, such as Britain, where the admiral of the *classis britannica*, Carausius, had made himself independent in AD286 – so it clearly represented a widespread trend.

THE NEW FORTRESSES

Typically these new fortresses had several common features: they had fewer entrances (often only one) guarded by a complex gatehouse that sometimes had a portcullis. They had massive projecting towers that allowed the archers, or soldiers operating the catapults now sometimes mounted on them, to cover the approaches. Their walls were much thicker and higher than those of earlier forts, sometimes up to 65ft (18m) high and 15ft (4.6m) thick. Finally, their ditches were wider and deeper and their berms (the strip between ditch and wall) wider. Old military camps were often adapted to the new fortress style, typically with fewer buildings inside, suggesting that they housed less forces, and that civilians may have sheltered inside the walls in times of invasion. It is also likely that these empty spaces sometimes sheltered mobile forces, the *comitatenses*, *en route* through the empire.

Some of the finest surviving examples of these massive new fortresses can be found on the Saxon Shore, the south-east coast of Britain that was fortified from the mid-3rd century AD onwards against

Above: On Constantine I's death, Constantine II and his brothers divided the empire in three.

the new threat from Saxon raiders. Portchester near Portsmouth, the best preserved, dates from the AD280s. Within its giant walls, still rising some 30ft (9m) above the estuary, a medieval church and castle nestle comfortably in opposite corners, with open fields between them. Along the Rhine, similarly huge structures were built to confront the new barbarian threats. The fortress at Deutz on the east (German) bank of the Rhine is typically imposing. Built by Constantine I in AD310 to defend Cologne, its 65ft (20m) walls were punctuated by even taller circular towers. At the other end of the empire, forts such as that at Qasr Bsheir in Jordan, built under Diocletian, were constructed with projecting towers to provide enfilading fire. Like medieval castles, such fortresses must have been defensible for long periods even by very small garrisons and could counter barbarian superiority in the field.

PSYCHOLOGICAL WARFARE
All these massive walls might suggest that Rome's enemies had become markedly more proficient in siege warfare. This was certainly true of the Sassanid Persians, who were far more determined and skilled fighters than the rather shambolic Parthian Arsacid dynasty they replaced. On the eastern frontier, long and complex

sieges became common. Those at Dura-Europos and Amida, where the Persians were victorious, and at Nisibis, where they were not, were typical. But the Romans built equally massive fortresses all along their northern frontiers, and very few barbarian tribes, if any, were ever good at proper sieges. But they would have certainly been impressed by these towering walls. So, in a more positive way, would the Roman soldiers inside them, especially as they were normally poorly trained and ill-equipped *limitanei* (frontier guards). Few Germans would have even attempted a siege against such an overwhelming example of Roman military engineering as Deutz. If they could not rush the castle by surprise or capture it by treachery – Rome itself only fell to the Visigoths when someone opened a gate to them – barbarian invaders would bypass them. This gave the Romans time to recover, to bring up forces from the mobile reserves and to stage a counter-attack. If the Romans could no longer overwhelm the barbarians by their unfailingly aggressive spirit, they could attempt to do so by their monumental fortifications.

Below: On the east coast of Kent, Richborough (Rutupiae) was the original Roman chief port of entry for Britain. Its fortifications were massively augmented in the later empire with huge walls, of which large sections still remain.

CITY WALLS

Above: The double walls around Constantinople (Istanbul) built by the emperor Theodosius II in the 5th century AD *still stand and have even been reconstructed for a small section. They repulsed attackers for 1,000 years.*

Below: The Porta Nigra (black gate) was the entrance, both ceremonial and fortified, to Trier, the capital of Gaul in the later empire. Its towers rise more than 70ft (20m).

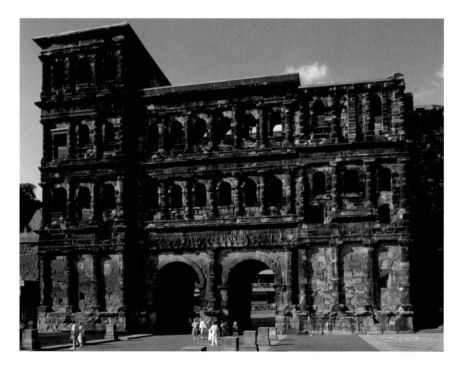

Since Augustus, Rome had been an open city, the Servian walls allowed to decay as they were engulfed by the growing capital. This reflected well-founded Roman confidence in its military prowess, which kept enemies safely distant. Similarly, cities in the provinces seldom needed walls unless on or near frontiers.

There were exceptions to this pacific norm, for older cities often retained their walls. Pompeii, far from any frontier, kept its boundary walls for ceremonial rather than military purposes, until Vesuvius destroyed it in AD79. In Boudicca's revolt in Britain, unwalled Colchester, London and St Albans were all sacked in AD61. So the Romans then built walls for a few towns, mostly those close to barbarous areas. But these walls, like those of the military camps, remained modest perimeters, gateways being more ceremonial than functional. However, further walls were added to London and other British cities after alarming barbarian attacks in AD193.

All this changed radically in the mid-3rd century AD. In the face of massive and repeated barbarian incursions, cities in near panic rushed to surround themselves with walls, using any materials that came to hand, including columns, tombstones and statues. Often these enclosed a far smaller area than before. Autun, for example, an important city in central Gaul, gave itself walls that covered only a third of its original area. Milan, for a time the capital of the western empire, enclosed less than 300 acres (120ha) within its new walls. Cities in the east did not shrink so much. Their walls were often restored, while in Britain the walls of London and York received progressively more massive fortifications but still protected the same areas. In Trier, which became the capital of Gaul and at times of the whole westernmost empire, gigantic walls protected an area of nearly 600 acres (240ha), making the walled city as large as it had ever been. Noteworthy at Trier is the ceremonial but also functional Porta Nigra (black gate), which has survived almost intact. Its two grand semicircular projecting towers rise to four tall floors over 70ft (20m) high and incorporate a portcullis, a device that went back centuries but which had become far more common. Trier remained impregnable until the whole of the Rhine frontier collapsed in AD406.

The walls Aurelian erected around Rome in the AD270s dwarfed those of all other western cities. Built chiefly of brick-faced concrete in great haste, the Aurelianic walls incorporate numerous pre-existing monuments such as the Pyramid of Cestius (a tomb), the walls of the Praetorian camp, the Porta Maggiore, part of Claudius' aqueduct and the small Amphitheatrum Castrense. About 20ft (6m) high and 12ft (3.6m) thick, they had square towers at about every 60yd (55m) with a platform for a catapult on top, while the major gateways had arched entrances flanked by twin semicircular towers. The entire circuit, covering most of Rome as it then was, was nearly

12 miles (19km) long and had 383 towers. Strengthened first by Valentinian I (AD364–75) and again by Honorius, it defied invaders until AD410, when treachery betrayed the landlocked city.

THE WALLS OF CONSTANTINOPLE

By far the grandest, most effective and best-preserved of late Roman city walls are the double (in some places triple) Theodosian walls of Constantinople, now Istanbul, the heart and head of the east Roman empire that metamorphosed into the Greek Byzantine empire. The walls were constructed between AD413 and AD437 in the reign of Theodosius II – a reaction to the sack of Rome. They replaced Constantine's shorter wall, which no longer contained the expanding city. The outer Theodosian walls were 20ft (6m) high with a deep moat in front of them. The inner walls were 40ft (12m) high, with 96 polygonal or square towers. The walls ran for almost 4 miles (6.4km) on the landward side of the peninsula and continued as a single wall right the way round the tip. On the other side of the Golden Horn, the small city of Pera was similarly defended, and a chain could be drawn across the harbour mouth to bar it to enemy ships. The walls defied all invaders – except for traitors – until 1453, when they finally fell to the Turkish besiegers' artillery. This probably makes them the most lastingly and consistently successful defences in history.

Above: The Porta Nigra (black gate) of Trier dates from the 4th century AD. Rising over 70ft (20m) the gate's twin towers incorporated a portcullis. It owes its remarkably good state of preservation to part of it being made into a chapel in the Middle Ages.

CHAPTER IV

THE GREAT WARS

More than any other factor it was war that helped to mould Roman society and its empire. Certain wars in particular propelled Rome first to dominance and then to absolute rule of the Mediterranean world: the wars against Carthage, in which Rome almost foundered; the wars in the eastern Mediterranean, which made Rome amazingly rich; and finally, Caesar's conquest of Gaul, which led to the expansion of Roman influence into northern Europe. Caesar's dazzling success was balanced by the more mixed results of Claudius' and Agricola's campaigns in Britain, which helped to link Britain with the Continent. But the unsuccessful wars in Germany left most of that country permanently outside the Roman *imperium* (empire), with momentous long-term consequences both for Germany and for Rome.

Civil wars helped to determine the form of government that Rome would have when ruling its new empire. As the empire matured, Rome reached something like its natural boundaries. From now on, any war would be defensive or, increasingly and catastrophically, internecine. The earlier great wars tend to be well recorded and provided some of the best examples of human conflict for many later generals and rulers. But the instrument of Rome's victories was always its army, unequalled both at marching and at fighting, relentlessly aggressive and willing to suffer almost any level of casualties if it led to final victory.

Left: Of all Rome's opponents, the most formidable was Hannibal, the Carthaginian general who invaded Italy.

MARCHING AND FIGHTING

By the late 2nd century BC, the Roman army had become the world's first large-scale, semi-permanent professional army, a status it maintained with relatively few changes for almost 400 years. In so doing, it developed fixed routines that struck contemporaries as formidably impressive. Flavius Josephus, writing around AD 70, repeats the admiring comments made by Polybius over two centuries earlier. The Romans organized their armies for their frequent marches, especially through hostile territory, in the same methodical way that they did everything else. When they engaged in actual combat, their relentless, controlled ferocity, coupled with a readiness to take high casualties if necessary, tended to overwhelm far larger numbers. This combination helped them to win their greatest wars.

Below: The sight of Roman legionaries marching in full armour towards them must have been intimidating to enemies, as these re-enactors demonstrate as they tramp along in formation.

When a full-sized Roman army was on the move, according to Josephus, it was preceded by light infantry and cavalry acting as scouts. Then came the vanguard, one legion plus cavalry, the legions drawing lots to decide which should be the vanguard – a prestigious if perilous position. Next came the camp surveyors, ten men detached from each century, followed by the pioneer corps, which had to remove obstacles in the army's path and build any necessary bridges. The general's and officers' baggage train came next, well protected by a strong mounted escort. Equally well protected behind it came the general himself, riding with his bodyguard of select cavalry and infantry. There followed the legionary cavalry, 120 for each legion, and then the mule trains carrying the numerous catapults and siege engines. According to Vegetius writing in the 4th century AD each century had its own *carroballista* (a light, bolt-shooting catapult) and each cohort had its own *onager* (a heavy stone-slinging catapult), so this mule train must have been large. Finally came the main body of the legions, all carrying their rations, camp-making tools and armour, marching six abreast. They were preceded by their *aquilifer* (eagle-bearer) and the trumpeters, and followed by their own baggage trains. A full legion of around 5,500 men must have spread for about a mile. Behind the legionaries marched the auxiliaries, with the rearguard composed of infantry and crack auxiliary cavalry. At the very end came the camp followers: wives, prostitutes, merchants and traders, including slave-dealers who could profit from Roman victory – slavery was the normal fate of any prisoners of war.

Roman armies were not as flamboyant or colourful as many Greek or Parthian forces, especially after Marius' reforms, when the richer soldiers stopped supplying their own armour. However, the well-drilled advance of up to 50,000 men – not such an uncommon number in the late Republic and Principate – must have been intimidatingly impressive.

BATTLE STATIONS

One of the advantages of the Roman *triplex acies* – the triple line of troops – was that troops did not have to fight to victory or to the death, but could be reinforced from the ranks behind. Unlike both the Greek *phalanx* and the Celtic-German mass, which relied on keeping the front ranks fighting until they triumphed by weight of numbers or else broke, this reduced the chances of panic. Iron discipline and rigorous drilling practice made complex manoeuvres second nature, even in the heat of battle. Their long, curved shields also helped to protect their comrades while moving backwards and forwards. But the *triplex acies* in no way softened the rigours of war. Centurions and the *optiones*, their

lieutenants, kept the men fighting, pushing them back into line and threatening cowardice with punishment.

In the Republic, legionaries had advanced shouting, banging their weapons against their shields. But by Caesar's time they kept silent until within almost 50ft (15m) of the enemy, when they yelled and threw their javelins in one broadside. Superb discipline allowed their dense formation to be maintained until the last minute. Then the soldiers fought close up, using the boss on their shields to punch the enemy in the face while they stabbed him with their *gladius*.

The centurions led their men aggressively, but even the generals stayed in close contact with their troops – to oversee fighting and to reward or punish individual soldiers. In close combat, when a gap was made in the enemy's line by killing several soldiers, a bravely determined legionary would fight his way into it. He was in extreme danger until joined by his comrades. But if enough managed to do so, the entire enemy line could start to buckle. Fighting at such close quarters was exhausting, both physically and psychologically, and the forces often used to break off at times, hurling abuse at each other from lines only a few yards apart, before re-engaging. Perseverance and stamina, more than spectacular individual exploits – coordinated so that the legion became one huge stabbing and thrusting machine – dominated and decided most battles. These were qualities Roman legionaries had in abundance.

Above: The Via Appia to the south of Rome. Good roads were a secret of Rome's success in conveying troops quickly to all parts of the empire.

Below: The Roman army marched along its empire's well-paved roads in sandals and boots. Army boots have been found in a number of places, including Vindolanda in Northumberland, England.

THE PUNIC WARS
264–146 BC

Above: Cannae, site of Rome's worst military disaster in 216 BC, when Hannibal annihilated a Roman army. But his victory did Hannibal little good in the longer term.

Below: At Cannae, Hannibal destroyed a numerically far superior army by thinning out his centre (blue) and letting it bend like a bow under Roman attack (red). Then his cavalry encircled the legions, driving them into a dense mass unable to wield their swords properly.

When Rome blundered into war with Carthage in 264 BC, it began an epic contest that would test its foundations. Carthage was a richer, larger and more sophisticated state than Rome. Its string of fortified bases stretched from Cadiz in Spain to Tripoli in Libya, and it was in the process of extending its control of Sicily. Greek observers must have expected it to contain, if not crush, what was still a farmers' republic. But Rome surprised the Greeks by its final victory over Carthage, which made it the dominant power first in the west Mediterranean and soon in the whole inland sea.

WAR AT SEA

The First Punic (Latin for Carthaginian) War was unusual for Rome as it was decided mostly at sea. Recognizing the need to counter Punic naval supremacy, the Romans quickly built fleets and defeated the Carthaginians with the *corvus*, the iron boarding device that let Romans fight as if on land. The *corvus* was a double-edged invention, however, as it made a galley top-heavy and many

fleets sank. Rome's victory in 241 BC was won by normal galleys. This was after Regulus had come to within a day's march of Carthage but was beaten by the Spartan general Xanthippus in 255 BC. Regulus was taken prisoner and sacrificed his life for his city, a patriotic act not atypical of Romans at the time.

ROMAN DEFEAT

Regulus may have been no military genius but, in the next war, Cornelius Scipio (later Africanus) was. This was fortunate for Rome, for Hannibal was a fearsome enemy whose daring was shown by his unprecedented choice of route over the Alps, and by his defeats of Roman armies at Ticino and Trebbia in the Po Valley in

218BC. After being ambushed in a mist, 30,000 Romans died. Hannibal, entering Italy on his one surviving elephant, defeated Rome again at Lake Trasimene in 217BC. He ignored the undefended road to Rome, perhaps because he lacked a siege train, but a year later annihilated Rome's biggest army yet – 80,000 men – at Cannae. Here Roman military amateurism was shown at its most inept. Trusting in their numbers, they let their central infantry push back the thin Punic infantry line. As Hannibal intended, this bent rather than broke, enveloping the enemy, while the superior Carthaginian cavalry, routing the Roman horsemen, circled round to attack from the rear. Packed so tightly that they could not fight, some Romans then fled but many more were cut down. Roman losses reputedly approached 70,000 that day.

When Hannibal's peace offers were rejected, the war became one of attrition and, despite the defection of some major cities like Capua, Rome here had the advantage. Hannibal could train his disparate troops, who included Spaniards, Gauls, Numidians, Samnites and other disaffected Italians, into a unified force, but he needed reinforcements, which never came. Meanwhile, Roman reserves of manpower – sources say over 700,000 – were readily available. Provided the Romans followed the unpopular scorched-earth tactics of Fabius Cunctator, their (emergency) dictator, they would win, even if at great cost to Italian agriculture.

SCIPIO IN SPAIN AND AFRICA

In the event, Rome counter-attacked, striking at Hannibal's base in Spain to prevent reinforcements reaching him. Scipio captured Cartagena in 209BC and defeated Hasdrubal's army at Baecula. Scipio finished off Carthaginian power at Ilpica in 206BC. In these battles he emulated Hannibal's encircling tactics to great effect. Despite the Senate's denial of adequate troops, he invaded Africa in 204BC and won over Massinissa of Numidia. With this fine Numidian

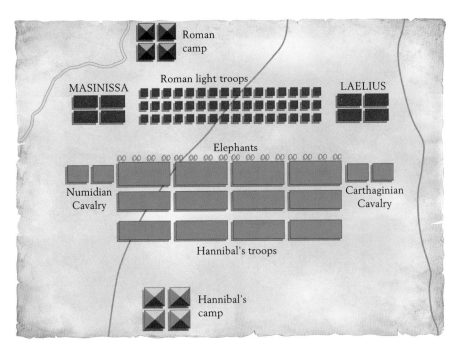

cavalry, Scipio finally defeated Hannibal at Zama in 202BC. The final battle between the two generals was a slogging match, Hannibal's many elephants being countered by Roman discipline, and was finally decided by Roman cavalry.

The Third Punic War of 149–146BC was an unequal and unnecessary contest. The Carthaginians, despite economic recovery, presented no military threat to a Rome still paranoid about Hannibal, but war was fomented by the Numidian king, encroaching on Carthaginian territory. It led to the final destruction of Carthage.

Above: The battle of Zama, which ended the Second Punic War, was won chiefly by the discipline of Roman legions after they had repelled Hannibal's elephants.

Below: Hannibal used elephants as tanks. But they were a two-edged weapon, easy for a coolly determined opponent to turn back or avoid, and liable to stampede in blind panic.

CONQUERING THE GREEKS
200–133BC

The eastern Mediterranean world conquered after 200BC appeared to many Romans as wealthy, sophisticated and alluring, but also effete and even dissolute. In a long series of wars, Alexander's generals, the *diaodochi* (successors), had created three powerful Greek-ruled kingdoms: the Antigonids in Macedonia, the Seleucids in Asia Minor, Syria and Mesopotamia, and the Ptolemies in Egypt and Palestine. These dominated the ancient world from the Adriatic to central Asia, but the cities of Greece proper remained independent and feuding. The recurrent wars between the great Hellenistic powers (as the expanded Greek world after Alexander the Great is known) were conducted in a relatively civilized, limited fashion, like those of the 18th century. Their professional but expensive armies relied mainly on spearmen massed into *phalanxes* and armed with sarissas, pikes up to 20ft (6m) long, supplemented by dashing cavalry with plumed helmets, fierce-looking chariots and many elephants. Such military splendours, however, especially the rigid formation of the *phalanx*, could not compete with the flexible maniples of battle-hardened Roman legions led by generals who had learnt their trade in the rigours of the Punic Wars. The Romans' brutally realistic attitude to war shocked the Greeks, who preferred to resort to diplomacy and negotiations rather than needless battles.

Philip V of Macedonia, a successful if impetuous ruler, unwisely allied himself with Hannibal after Cannae, partly because Rome had annexed nearby south Illyria. This First Macedonian War fizzled out in 205BC but Rome did not forget Philip's action. Urged on by smaller Greek states anxious that Philip's alliance with the Seleucid Antiochus III threatened their independence, Rome sent Flaminius in 200BC to drive the Macedonians from Greece proper. At the battle of Cynoscephalae in 197BC, Flaminius displayed the flexibility pioneered by Scipio Africanus to defeat Philip, his maniples outflanking the clumsy *phalanx* on what was admittedly mountainous ground. Macedonian power in Greece was ended, though Macedonia itself was not destroyed, and Flaminius promised the delighted southern Greek cities liberty. It was to prove a hollow promise, for he meant self-rule as subordinate allies, not full freedom.

KING OF KINGS
Antiochus III was still undefeated, however. A capable and highly ambitious monarch, he appeared to Rome to be recreating Alexander's vast empire, for not only had he reconquered much of central Asia, but he menaced both Egypt and Europe, and was calling himself King of Kings. Even worse, Hannibal, exiled from Carthage, was now a guest at Antiochus' court. In 192BC Antiochus sent a small force into Greece proper to help the Aetolians, disgruntled by the

Above: Athens, though no longer important politically, also suffered in the wars that marked Rome's conquest of Greece. Later it became the empire's university town.

Below: The theatre on the Acropolis of Pergamum, the capital of the wealthy Attalid kingdom, Rome's chief ally in the Greek world.

THE TANKS OF ANTIQUITY

When the Romans first encountered elephants in Pyrrhus' army in 280BC, they were panic-stricken. But they soon learnt to deal with these armoured giants by opening their ranks to let them through, or by repelling them by javelin volleys. In war elephant charges could inflict terrible damage upon infantry that panicked, while their smell drove horses unused to them mad with fear. But elephants were a double-edged weapon, for they in turn were easy to panic and could turn against their own armies. Because of this, mahouts, their riders, carried hammers and chisels to kill them if needed.

The Hellenistic monarchs used Indian elephants, who were more easily trained and came from the elephant stud farm the Seleucids had established in Syria. But Hannibal and other Carthaginians used the North African forest elephant (now extinct), which was ridden like a horse. The Romans occasionally also deployed elephants in their armies, impressing enemies unused to them. However, they chiefly used them for animal and hunting displays, slaughtering them in large numbers in games to amuse the Roman populace.

recent settlement. This roused Roman wrath and they sent an army to defeat it the next year at Thermopylae. Rome followed this up with a naval victory and landed troops in Asia Minor for the final conflict at Magnesia in Asia Minor in 190BC.

For this deciding battle, Antiochus mobilized huge forces of over 70,000 men, including heavy Persian-style *cataphract* cavalry and large numbers of war elephants and chariots. However, the core of his army remained the *phalanx*. This formation, 32-men deep, bristled with spears and was almost invincible to frontal assault. Scipio Africanus was an unofficial adviser to his brother, the

nominal Roman commander, but Scipio himself was ill on the day of the battle. The key role in the battle was taken by Eumenes of Pergamum, a Hellenistic ally of Rome, whose heavy cavalry routed the Seleucid *cataphracts* and then returned to attack the Seleucid infantry in the rear. The Seleucid chariot and elephant charges had been repulsed earlier by the Roman legions, but the Macedonian *phalanx*, 16,000 strong, stood firm against Roman attacks until their stampeding elephants, panicked by Roman javelins, broke up their ranks. Finally, the Pergamene cavalry was able to surround the remaining Seleucid forces.

This defeat proved decisive. Antiochus had to pay a huge indemnity, withdraw completely from Asia Minor and expel Hannibal. The Seleucids were never again a great Mediterranean power. The Romans, as was their custom at the time, made no new provinces but gave the western Seleucid territories mostly to Eumenes, whose last descendant bequeathed them to Rome in 133BC. However, the Romans were now incontestably masters of the eastern Mediterranean too. Later Roman wars in Greece merely confirmed Roman supremacy, and this was challenged seriously only when Rome itself was divided at the time of Mithradates.

Above: A Roman legionary with a long oval shield and plumed helmet.

Below: Hannibal and his elephants fighting a Roman legion in north Italy, after the school of Raphael.

CAESAR'S CONQUEST OF GAUL
58–50 BC

Above: The siege of Alesia in 52BC, where the Gallic leader Vercingetorix had retreated, was the final battle in Caesar's conquest of Gaul.

Below: Caesar built a double wooden wall around the fortress at the siege of Alesia, to keep the Gauls in and prevent their relief army of 80,000 men breaking through.

Caesar's proconsular command in 58BC, for the exceptionally long term of five years, included Cisalpine Gaul (the Po valley) and Transalpine Gaul (southern France) with Greek cities at Marseilles and Antibes, a Roman colony at Narbonne and, lining the Rhône valley, various Celtic tribes. The vagueness of this northern frontier allowed Caesar, keen to rival Pompey's eastern conquests, to intervene far beyond his province. The Helvetii trying to migrate to the Atlantic, gave him an excuse. A series of bitter, genocidal wars resulted in all Gaul (France, Belgium, the Rhineland and western Switzerland) being conquered and Romanized. This conquest led to the extension of Roman power northwards and the enrichment of Caesar. In the long term it produced the civilization of France. This makes it among the most significant conquests in history.

The Celtic world Caesar destroyed was underestimated by classical writers because it lacked cities and literacy. But the Gauls were skilled metal workers, producing striking stylized artworks. They were great horsemen and had many types of carriage, while the Veneti in Brittany were fine mariners. The Gauls were also pioneers of the wheeled plough. Above all, they had an acute poetic and religious sense. Most of what we know of Celtic life comes from biased writers such as Caesar; only echoes of Celtic legends survive in Welsh and Irish poetry. However, the Gauls were fatally disunited politically, with about 60 separate states in 58BC. Caesar easily recruited Gallic cavalry to fight their fellow countrymen.

Caesar swiftly crushed the Helvetii at Armecy in 58BC, killing tens of thousands, forcing the survivors back to Switzerland. The next year, he attacked Ariovistus, a German king who had crossed into Gaul. Caesar routed the Germans in Alsace and then turned on the Belgae, living north of the Seine. In 57BC he also crushed the Nervi in Artois before other Belgae had mobilized, a victory that made him arbiter of Gaul. With his command renewed at Lucca in 56BC, Caesar returned to find that the Veneti in Brittany, angered by his proposed invasion of Britain, had revolted. Building a fleet, he defeated them at Quiberon Bay. Early in 55BC he repelled another German invasion even more brutally, building a timber bridge across the Rhine, a feat that stunned opinion in Rome.

Caesar's two "invasions" of Britain in 55BC and 54BC were also intended as propaganda. The first attack was a near disaster: many ships were damaged by tides that Caesar had not anticipated and he himself returned home after only 18 days. The next year he returned with a far larger force of five legions and 2,000 cavalry and forced Cassivellaunus, ruler of the Catuvellauni, the most powerful southern British tribe, to submit after storming his capital. But the conquest proved illusory: the Britons rejected Roman suzerainty as soon as Caesar left. Meanwhile, there was rebellion in Gaul.

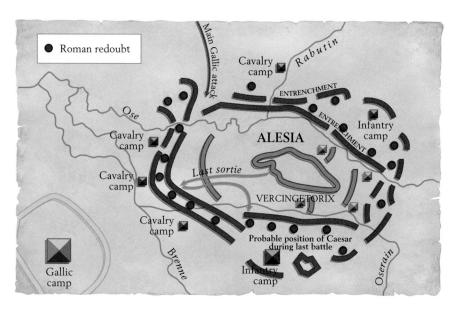

● Roman redoubt

Main Gallic attack

Rabutin

Cavalry camp

ENTRENCHMENT

Ose

ENTRENCHMENT

Infantry camp

Cavalry camp

ALESIA

Cavalry camp

Last sortie

VERCINGETORIX

Cavalry camp

Probable position of Caesar during last battle

Brenne

Oserain

Infantry camp

Gallic camp

*Left: Caesar's conquest of Gaul
was marked by numerous
campaigns of lightning rapidity
that overwhelmed the far more
numerous Gauls before they
had time to mobilize. His
legions marched from the Rhine
– which they bridged – to the
Atlantic, on which they sailed,
and back with a speed that
stunned Romans and Gauls
alike. (Only the Britons were
unimpressed.) But the conquest
of Gaul was only settled by
the drawn-out siege of Alesia.*

*Below: Vercingetorix, last and
greatest war leader of the
Gauls, shown heroically on
horseback. His scorched-earth
tactics were less heroic, but
they nearly defeated Caesar,
whose troops lived off the land
and who could not capture
Alesia by direct assault.*

THE SIEGE OF ALESIA

In 52BC the Gauls united behind a single leader, Vercingetorix of the Arverni in central Gaul. He decided to defeat Caesar by a scorched-earth policy to deny him supplies – the Roman army lived off the land – refusing direct battle. He drew them into central Gaul where Caesar suffered a defeat attacking the fortress of Gerovia, which encouraged other tribes to join the revolt. But Vercingetorix mistakenly retreated behind the walls of Alesia with 90,000 men, thinking it was impregnable. Caesar recognized that it was "on the crown of a hill high enough for blockade to be the only means of capturing it". He built a huge double line of walls, an example of bi-circumvallation, about 14 miles (22km), to starve the Gauls

– who included women and children – into surrender. The 80,000-strong Gallic relief army failed to break through Caesar's lines, fortified by iron-tipped spikes dug into the ground. In desperation, Vercingetorix tried three times to break out before surrendering in late 52BC. This ended the Gallic wars.

The Romans showed no mercy to the Gauls, killing about a third of the Gallic population in the wars. Caesar won by his lightning rapidity and the discipline of his legions. The conquered land was later divided into three provinces (Aquitainia in the south-west, Lugdunensis in the centre and Belgica in the north-east) and assessed for tribute. Ultimately, Gaul would prove the most receptive and fruitful of all Rome's conquests.

THE LAST CIVIL WARS: 49–30BC

Above: A statue of Pompey, showing him posing rather improbably as a god or hero. He was, however, an excellent general and statesmanlike in foreign affairs. But in Roman politics he could never decide which faction to support, a fatal indecisiveness.

Below: Major battle sites of the last civil wars.

Fresh from his conquest of Gaul, in January 49BC Caesar had the best army: experienced, loyal, large – ten legions – and to hand. By contrast, his adversary Pompey's best troops were in Spain and out of practice. Caesar had no wish to start another civil war; memories of the conflict between Marius and Sulla were still fresh in the public mind. His enemies in the Senate tried to divest him of his Gallic command and refused to let him stand for consul *in absentia*. If he returned to Italy as a private citizen he faced immediate prosecution that would end his political career, if not his life. According to Suetonius, as he hesitated on the banks of the river Rubicon marking the borders of Italy, a ghostly figure appeared from the twilight and crossed over. Caesar then moved into Italy with his army – an act of treason – and triggered civil war.

With just one legion, Caesar raced down the east coast to Brindisi but failed to catch Pompey and his other opponents before they left for Greece, where Pompey had huge support. Before turning east, Caesar crushed the Pompeian forces in Spain at Lerida. In 48BC he crossed to Greece, eluding Pompey's numerous ships. Antony joined Caesar three months later with reinforcements, but attempts to blockade Pompey's base at Durrachium (Durazzo) failed disastrously. Pompey out-walled him and he withdrew.

The deciding battle took place in Thessaly on 6 June 48BC at Pharsalus. It was probably the largest battle ever fought between Romans; Pompey had 80,000 troops and was strong in cavalry, but most of his infantry were out of condition. Caesar had fewer men but all were skilled, hardened veterans. The brilliant discipline of Caesar's legionaries, who advanced with their *pila* (javelins) as pikes, countered Pompey's cavalry's initially successful charge. By attacking their flank, the legions drove Pompey's horsemen back. Pompey was killed soon after in Egypt.

✕ Battle site

*Right: Actium, last battle of the civil wars,
was decided at sea when Antony's fleet,
trying to escape the blockade, was defeated.*

With great speed, Caesar won many
other battles around the Mediterranean.
But he was less good at establishing peace.
After his assassination in 44BC, civil war
flared up again between his assassins, led
by Brutus and Cassius, and his supporters,
Antony and Octavian. The two battles of
Philippi in 42BC were won by Antony,
who went on to rule the eastern half of
the empire and pursue his relationship
with Cleopatra. Inevitably, the two dynasts
moved towards a renewal of war by 32BC.

ACTIUM: THE LAST BATTLE

Despite Octavian's lurid propaganda
campaign, Antony was still popular with
his own troops. He also had Cleopatra's
wealth, which could give him a fleet, as
well as promises of support from many
eastern client kings, including Herod the
Great. Octavian had the recruiting grounds
of Italy, and a very good general in his
friend Agrippa. Once again the rivals
converged on Greece, Agrippa slipping
across the Adriatic in the winter of 31BC,
followed by Octavian in the spring. But
Antony made a mistake when he took
Cleopatra with him to western Greece.
His own men began to believe Octavian's
propaganda about their general and began
to desert. The final battle took place on
2 September 31BC when Antony led his
fleet in an attempted breakout Although
he had many quinqueremes and more
troops, Antony's fleet was defeated by
Agrippa's, which used smaller, swifter
Liburnian galleys. Antony broke off the
battle, following Cleopatra's flight to Egypt.
Many of his supporters then surrendered.
The following year, Antony and Cleopatra
committed suicide when the Caesarean
troops entered Alexandria, so ending the
last Roman civil war for a century.

*Right: At Pharsalus, Caesar's more
disciplined but outnumbered troops defeated
Pompey's army by flank attacks.*

ALONG THE ELBE: 12BC–AD16

Although Caesar had proclaimed the Rhine as the natural, almost inevitable, north-west frontier of the empire, this was not so evident to his successor Augustus. Germanic tribes had already infiltrated west of the river into Gallia Belgica, the north-eastern Gallic province. Further, a German invasion in 17BC by the Sugambri and Isupetes tribes, which had defeated the Romans under Lollius, called for revenge. Augustus, confident after victories in northern Iberia (23BC), the Alpine provinces (16–15BC) and the Balkans (13–9BC), saw no reason to halt the expansion of the empire on this frontier.

Rome's geographical knowledge of northern Europe became more vague the further east it looked, but the tribes between the Elbe and the Rhine did not appear exceptionally formidable. It seemed that Germania could be conquered and pacified as easily as Gaul, a considerably larger, more populous area. A frontier along the Elbe to the Danube would eliminate the awkward upper Rhine–Danube junction, and shorten the whole frontier by almost 300 miles (480km).

There were differences between the two lands, however. If thought barbarous by Greeks and Romans, *Gallia comata* (long-haired Gaul), beyond Rome's old Mediterranean province, had been wealthy and dynamic in its rural way; its fertile land had supported advanced farming. Western Germany, by contrast, had thin soils with heavy, dark forests and many bogs and heaths. Partly because of this, the German tribes were less well developed and less settled than those of Gaul or Britain and their shifting settlements were less easily controlled. But such differences were not then apparent to the Romans.

Accordingly, Augustus ordered an advance to the Elbe, with troops commanded by his stepson Drusus in 12BC, while his other stepson, Tiberius, finally pacified the Pannonian plain. Although Drusus' fleet was wrecked by tides in the Zuyder Zee (his men were saved only by his Frisian allies), in three successive campaigning seasons his armies still advanced up the Main and Lippe valleys towards the Elbe.

Drusus' death in 9BC meant that Tiberius replaced him before retiring in 6BC from public life, in presumed disgust at Augustus' open preference for his grandsons. The German campaigns at first seem to have progressed slowly but steadily, even without Tiberius. Very soon traders and tax-collectors, in the normal pattern, entered the region, which began to be organized and taxed as a province. However, a reaction to the Roman advance led to the formation of a powerful Marcomanni kingdom in Bohemia. To deal with this threat, in AD6 a two-pronged invasion of the area was planned from the Rhine and the Danube. Tiberius, back from voluntary exile in Rhodes, was about to strike north from near Vienna with a huge force of 12 legions when news came of a massive revolt in Pannonia and he turned east. The gruelling war that followed, "the most serious

Above: The Elbe in north Germany proved a frontier too far for the Romans after the disaster that befell Varus and his legions in AD9.

Below: The "Gemma Augustea" shows Augustus and the goddess Roma receiving Tiberius, who, if charmless, was a very fine general.

of all our foreign wars since the Punic wars", according to Suetonius, distracted him. Meanwhile, there was disaster in Germany proper.

THE VARUS DISASTER

Quinctilius Varus, who commanded three legions in north-west Germany, was less a soldier than an administrator, although he had suppressed a revolt in Judaea as governor of Syria in 4BC. Hastening in to deal with a revolt by the Cherusci, one of the German tribes, in AD9, his army was ambushed in the Teutoburg Forest near Osnabrück. Varus had been betrayed by the Cherusci king Arminius (Hermann), supposedly a Roman ally. Surrounded by Germans, Varus committed suicide and his three legions were lost. The whole Roman position east of the Rhine began to unravel rapidly. Back in Rome, the aged emperor Augustus was crushed by the news. He ordered special patrols around the city, reputedly banging his head against the wall and crying, "Quinctilius Varus, give me back my legions!"

In fact, the other German tribes did not join the Cherusci (the Marcomanni in particular quarrelled with them) and there was no general attack across the river Rhine. However, Tacitus was right when he referred to the Cherusci king Arminius as "the liberator of Germany", for his revolt marked the end of real Roman attempts to subjugate Germany. Drusus' son, Germanicus, led a series of major punitive raids over the Rhine, in AD15 finding and burying the bones of Varus' legions, and the following year sailing up the river Ems to defeat the Cherusci in a set battle.

However, Tiberius, the new emperor, then recalled Germanicus. Tiberius preferred to rely on diplomacy and bribes to control the German tribes. This was successful, for Arminius was soon killed in a conspiracy by his own people. The frontier then became established on the Rhine, and northern and central Germany remained permanently outside the Roman empire, although influenced by trade and other contacts with it.

Above: The attempted Roman conquest of Germany.

Below: The Rhine offered a convenient frontier for the Romans along much of its length but was not impassable.

THE CONQUEST OF LOWLAND BRITAIN: AD43–70

Above: The bookish emperor Claudius proved remarkably successful as a conqueror, adding lowland Britain to the empire in what appeared a relatively simple campaign. But the island was not at first a great asset to the empire.

Below: The hill fort at Badbury Rings, Dorset, was one of the many oppida, *or fortified British townships, that the Romans stormed in their initial conquest of Britain.*

Paradoxically, one of the most professional of Rome's military campaigns was carried out at the orders of one of its least military emperors, Claudius. This was no coincidence. Aware he lacked the soldiering experience of a Roman aristocrat, Claudius needed to conquer Britain. His predecessor, Caligula, had massed troops on the Channel as if for an invasion but ordered them to throw javelins at the sea, according to Suetonius. But Claudius was serious. The uncomfortable, marginally dangerous journey he made north for the surrender of Colchester (Camulodonum) shows the importance he attached to this campaign.

Ever since Julius Caesar had invaded and misleadingly claimed that he had conquered Britain in 55–54BC, the island had intrigued the Romans. It had a reputation – overrated, it turned out – of being rich in gold, and the south was inhabited by tribes like the Belgae related to those in Gaul. The Gallic connection was a reason for invasion, for the Druids reputedly helped keep alive Gallic hostility to Rome. Another excuse was that Caratacus, an heir of King Cunobelin (Cymbeline), had attacked Verica, who appealed to Rome for help. Prestige was, however, the chief reason for the invasion. It was 40 years since Rome had gained a major new province.

Four legions were mustered under Aulus Plautius, 40,000 men including auxiliaries. Despite a mutiny by troops alarmed at embarking for an unknown land, they landed safely at Richborough, and after two days' bitter fighting defeated the Britons at the Medway. Another victory followed when the Romans crossed the Thames. Plautius, impressed by British resistance, halted the advance until the emperor could arrive with reinforcements, which included some elephants. Then Claudius watched his troops storm Colchester, the Catuvellaunian capital, and declared it the capital of the new province (and six years later, a Roman colony), before returning home to celebrate a triumph.

Plautius continued the swift conquest. Vespasian, commanding the Second Legion, struck south-west, capturing 20 *oppida* (tribal strongholds). Meanwhile, the Fourteenth Legion advanced north-west and the Ninth Legion moved north. Within four years a provisional line was established along the Fosse Way from Lincoln to Exeter. Tribes such as the Iceni and the Brigantes became client kings, shielding the new province. This began to fill with Roman merchants and adventurers. But Caratacus escaped to continue resistance in the Welsh hills.

Plautius' successor, Ostorius Scapula, tried to strengthen the new province by disarming all tribes south of the Fosse and pushing the frontier closer to Wales. Caratacus, defeated in battle, took refuge with Cartimandua, Queen of the Brigantes, who handed him over to the Romans in AD51. Caratacus was paraded through Rome but pardoned by Claudius.

Left: Claudius' invasion of Britain at first restricted itself to the south-east of the island, with a possible provisional frontier along the Fosse Way and a capital at Colchester, although campaigns further west were needed to hunt down Caratacus. But the Romans soon found themselves drawn into Wales to suppress the Druids in AD60, and then Cerialis had to march north to control the large but troubled kingdom of the Brigantes.

The conquest did not, however, go so smoothly as it approached upland Britain. The Brigantes' kingdom was riven by disputes; Cartimandua was driven out by her consort after a disagreement and had to be reinstated by the Romans. Rome's real efforts, under the new governor Suetonius Paulinus, focused on subduing Anglesey, centre of political and religious resistance. The Romans crossed the Menai Straits and overran the island, cutting down the sacred Druidical groves. Then, suddenly, the whole province was endangered by a new revolt.

BOUDICCA'S REVOLT
The last Iceni king, Prasutagus, had made the emperor co-heir with his two daughters. But a venal procurator, Decianus Catus, and his loathed *publicani* seized land and goods. When Boudicca, the widowed queen, was flogged by Romans and her daughters raped, the Iceni rose in revolt. Joined by the Trinovantes, the Britons sacked Colchester and moved on London. Paulinus hurried with a few troops to London. Realizing he could not defend an unwalled city, he withdrew, "undeflected by the prayers and tears of those who begged for his help", in Tacitus' words. The Britons sacked London and St Albans, reportedly killing 70,000 people. Paulinus defeated them near Towcester – according to Tacitus, 80,000 Britons were killed and 400 Romans. Paulinus took a terrible vengeance, even on Britons who had stayed neutral. But before the whole province was devastated, Paulinus was checked by the intervention of Julius Classicianus, the new procurator. Of partly Gallic descent, Classicianus recognized the Britons' real problems and his report led to Paulinus being replaced by the more conciliatory Turpilianus. These two pacified the province so effectively the south never rose again.

Below: Queen Boudicca, who traditionally led her people, the Iceni, in a revolt that nearly ended Roman rule in all Britain.

AGRICOLA'S NORTHERN CAMPAIGNS: AD79–84

Above: Although Agricola marched far up the east coast of Scotland, the Romans did not penetrate the highlands proper, such as Glen Quoich.

Under Agricola, the Romans certainly came closer to conquering all Britain than at any other time. According to Tacitus, Agricola's completion of the conquest was prevented only by the jealousy of the emperor Domitian, who recalled him just as final victory was in sight. *"Perdomita Britannia et statim missa"* (Britain was completely conquered and at once let go), he commented sourly. But Tacitus was Agricola's son-in-law and shared the aristocracy's general hatred of Domitian. Just how feasible such a conquest was remains debatable, and Domitian did have valid reasons for recalling some legions.

When Agricola, who had just been a consul, arrived in Britain as governor, probably in late AD78, he was returning to a province he had fought in as a young man. Taking command of his old Twentieth Legion, then based at Viriconium (Wroxeter), he immediately went on the offensive against the Ordovices of mid-Wales and almost annihilated them. He built forts at Caernarvon and other places in north Wales, but also began "encouraging wild men who lived in scattered settlements… to live in a peaceful manner. Agricola … helped them officially to build temples, *fora* [market places] and private houses… and had the children of important Britons educated in civilized ways", recorded Tacitus. Many Britons now became Romanized, as the numerous buildings of this Flavian period show.

Right: Agricola's campaign, possibly intended to complete the conquest of Britain, started with a two-pronged attack on each flank of the Pennines. Once into what is now southern Scotland, his armies united to push up the east coast, establishing a line of forts centring on the new legionary camp at Inchtuthil. Roman victory in the supposedly decisive battle of Mons Graunpius – the site has yet to be determined – in fact did not conclude the conquest. The Caledonians vanished into the highland mists and soon after Agricola himself was recalled, his forts being abandoned a few years later.

Agricola's campaign in Scotland AD 78–84

Battle of Mons Graupius AD 83 (suggested locations)

NORTH SEA

CALEDONII

VENICONES

Tay

Fort at Inchtuthil abandoned AD 87

Inchtuthil

Forth

Agricola advances to the river Tay AD 79

Antonine Wall

DUMNONII

Clyde

VOTADINI

SELGOVAE

Romans control southwest Scotland AD 79

NOVANTAE

Tyne

Hadrian's Wall

In AD79 Agricola sent two large columns of troops up each side of the Pennines, overawing the Brigantes and reaching the Tyne–Solway line. The next year he pressed on to the Forth. Reuniting his armies, he then marched north again, building forts as he went. A provisional line across Scotland, from the Clyde to the Forth, was probably established and he campaigned in south-west Scotland. Looking across to Ireland, he estimated that its conquest would require only one legion – suggesting wild optimism or poor geography on his part. However, north-east Scotland drew him back. In summer AD82 or 83 he moved north with a supporting fleet through increasingly hostile territory with the permission of the new emperor, Domitian. The Ninth Legion was almost destroyed when it became detached from the main army. At Mons Graupius (probably near Inverness), Agricola's army finally met the main Caledonian forces mustered under King Calgacus. According to Tacitus, these northern Britons had about 30,000 men. This was far more than Agricola's forces, which included auxiliaries, among them some Britons. Although the Caledonians had the advantage of the slope and a prepared position, Roman discipline overcame Celtic courage. Reportedly, 10,000 Caledonians were killed for only 360 Romans, although 20,000 Caledonians escaped. These figures may exaggerate the extent of the victory, but Scotland did seem truly conquered.

Agricola ordered the construction of a full-scale legionary camp for the Twentieth Legion at Inchtuthil, the largest of a chain of forts that stretched almost from the Moray Firth to Loch Lomond. A fleet went north to circumnavigate Britain and confirm it really was an island. Agricola was presumably planning another campaign to the extreme north, but Domitian recalled him. Problems on the Danube meant reinforcements were needed. About AD86 Inchtuthil and other forts north of the Clyde–Forth line were dismantled and Rome's advance into Scotland abandoned.

The Highlands were left untamed, indeed untouched, despite Tacitus' claims to the contrary, and the southern uplands were still disputed. From unconquered Scotland would later come many of the tribes that would threaten Roman Britain.

BETWEEN TWO WALLS

The northern frontier remained unsettled until the famous visit of the emperor Hadrian in AD122. Hadrian generally favoured easily defensible frontiers, even if this entailed some withdrawal, and he now chose the line along the Tyne to the Solway for his great wall. At first built partly in turf and timber, it was soon wholly consolidated in stone, requiring the excavation in total of some 2 million tons of rock and soil. It was ultimately the most imposing fortification in the empire. However, this did not mean that the Romans rejected all interests or control north of the wall. Patrols and forts, such as Newstead on the Tweed, were maintained well to the north. In AD139 under Antoninus Pius, the frontier was advanced to the waist of Scotland again and a new turf wall some 37 miles (59km) long was built. This was the Antonine Wall, about 100 miles (160km) north of the existing line. Hadrian's Wall was not completely abandoned, but some of its gates were removed. However, an uprising led to the abandonment of the Antonine Wall in the early AD150s. It was reoccupied and finally abandoned again and dismantled in AD162. Hadrian's Wall again became the frontier, but due to Rome's civil wars it was overrun in the AD190s, with tribesmen raiding as far as York. To restore the situation, Septimius Severus visited Britain in person and twice invaded Scotland, perhaps reaching the Moray Firth. But when he died at York in AD211 his sons abandoned his planned conquests. Hadrian's Wall, substantially repaired, once again became the frontier of Roman Britain. Beyond it, the Caledonians began to organize themselves into threatening confederacies that would soon ravage the south.

Above: An emblem of the Twentieth Legion, once commanded by Agricola, which spear-headed his new campaign.

Below: Ruins of a granary at Housesteads on Hadrian's Wall.

TRAJAN AND THE CONQUEST OF DACIA

Above: Battle scene between the Dacians and the Romans from the Ludovisi Sarcophagus. The wars of AD101–6, which removed a threatening enemy and gained much gold, proved to be Rome's last wholly profitable war of conquest.

Below: A river ferry passes the Iron Gates on the Danube, the great gorge that divides the river. The Romans built a road along the south cliff face.

Trajan (reigned AD98–117) was the last emperor to expand the empire significantly. If his wars in Asia proved a costly failure, his conquest of Dacia was a triumphant success. It led to the removal of a significant threat on the river Danube, a huge gain in booty for the Roman treasury and, despite Roman withdrawal 170 years later, to the enduring creation of the only Latin people in eastern Europe: the Romanians.

Dacia, a mountain-ringed, fertile and gold-rich land, had been a powerful, centralized kingdom under a ruler called Burebista in Caesar's time. Its people were renowned as fighters and skilled metallurgists and engineers, and had developed their own coinage. In AD85 Dacia acquired a brilliant new leader in Decebalus, who called himself High King. He may have had some experience of Roman military life, for he began organizing a powerful army on Roman lines. Twenty years of war followed – they proved among the fiercest Rome ever fought in Europe.

Domitian at once sent an army under Cornelius Fuscus to repel Dacian incursions, but it was humiliatingly defeated. Calling in legions from Britain and elsewhere, the Romans mounted a further campaign that won a victory at Tapae (near Turnu Severin) in AD88. However, the revolt of Antoninus Saturninus, the legate of upper Germany, in January AD89 meant that the troops had to deal with threatened civil war. The result was an uneasy truce. Domitian concentrated on containing the Dacian threat, quelling the tribes in Pannonia and building an earthwork across the Dobrudja, between the Danube and Tomis on the Black Sea, to prevent Dacian raids at this marshy extremity.

Trajan, who became emperor in AD98, was an experienced soldier. He boosted the Roman army's strength to perhaps 400,000 by recruiting two legions, besides doubling the size of the first cohort in each and adding new auxiliary forces. Seeing how Dacian power and pride were continuing to grow he decided to deal with the Dacians. With other frontiers peaceful, he concentrated 13 legions plus auxiliaries (*c*.130,000 men) on the lower Danube. He crossed the river at the head of this force in AD101.

The wars, vividly recorded on Trajan's Column in Rome, lasted five years. The first led to an inconclusive victory, with Decebalus accepting humiliating terms. Trajan now prepared for a larger invasion by having Apollodorus build his bridge across the Danube and construct a road through the Iron Gates Gorge. Here the river narrowed between cliffs and the armies were able to march all the way along the Danube. The war resumed in AD105 and the final attack in AD106 overwhelmed the Dacian capital of Sarmizegetusa Regia. Decebalus committed suicide. His head later graced Trajan's triumph, along with a huge quantity of gold, the last really significant war spoils in Rome's history.

On the map, the new province – which lengthened the imperial frontiers by some 350 miles (560km) – looked vulnerable. However, on the ground the reality was rather different. By projecting Roman power to the edge of the Eurasian steppe, Trajan made it easier to control the Sarmatian, Carpi and Iazyges tribes on either side. A line of defences along the great mountain wall of the Carpathians, the *limes Porolissensis*, protected the new province with auxiliary-garrisoned forts. These were linked by watchtowers and backed by the Thirteenth Legion stationed at Apulum, reaching a total of 30–40,000 men (about the same as Britain). Dacia itself was settled by Romans, and the gold mines, an imperial monopoly, were profitably exploited.

THE PROVINCE ABANDONED

Hadrian is said to have contemplated abandoning the new province completely. This would have been in keeping with his general policy of retrenchment, although jealousy of Trajan's success could also have played a part; his destruction of the amazing Danubian bridge Apollodorus

had built seems pettily negative. But he was dissuaded by the pleas of the colonists themselves – the productive gold mines may have swayed him too – and he evacuated only the Banat plain to the west of the province, which was vulnerable to raids from Sarmatian tribesmen. Over the following century, the whole middle and lower Danubian area, from modern Budapest down to the Black Sea, prospered and became Romanized and increasingly urbanized. It was to provide vital reservoirs of troops – and emperors – in the 3rd century. One of these Illyrian emperors, Aurelian, accepting that Dacia was no longer defensible against new enemies such as the Goths and Gepids, finally evacuated it in AD270, settling its Latin-speaking inhabitants in a new province, Dacia, south of the Danube (approximately northern Serbia). However, some Latin-speaking Dacians must have survived the endless waves of invasion, probably sheltering in the Carpathians to re-emerge centuries later, still speaking their basically Romance language.

Above: The inauguration at Dobrela of the bridge over the Danube, which was built by Apollodorus for Trajan.

Below: Trajan's Column in Rome still proclaims his many victories.

TRAJAN AND THE EAST

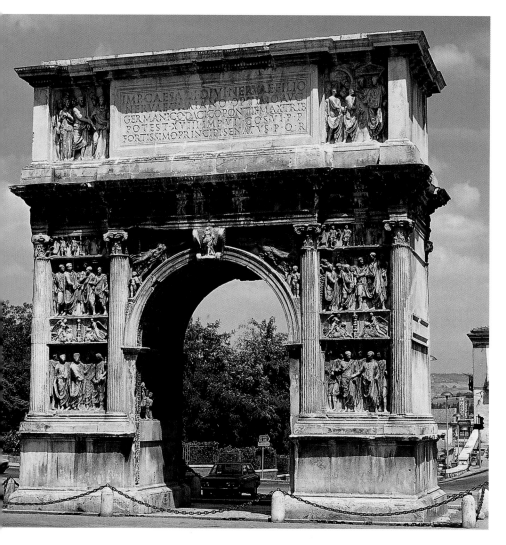

Above: The Parthians relied heavily on horse archers such as this one, about to fire his recurved composite bow.

Below: Trajan's triumphal arch at Benevento, Italy.

Ever since Pompey had marched through Asia in the 60s BC, many Romans had dreamt of eastern conquests. There was widespread admiration for Alexander the Great, who had conquered the Persians *en route* to India. Parthia, the successor to the eastern Persian empire from the Euphrates to central Asia, was a ramshackle, semi-feudal monarchy, which was often unable to control its nobles and which evoked little loyalty from its varied subjects in Mesopotamia (Iraq).

There were more material reasons for invading Parthia and trying to annex at least its richest part, Mesopotamia. The great Hellenistic city of Seleucia-on-the-Tigris (opposite Baghdad) still flourished. In the 1st century AD the city had a population of *c.*600,000, almost as big as Alexandria's. Mesopotamia was very fertile, while its cities' trade with India reputedly surpassed Syria's. The ancient "Fertile Crescent", from the Gulf to the Mediterranean, had often been ruled by one monarch, most recently by the Hellenistic Seleucids. There was no good reason why it should not be again.

Augustus had prudently disappointed Roman expectations that he would revenge the Parthian defeats of Crassus (in 53BC) and Antony (in 36BC). Instead, by a peaceful agreement in 20BC Rome received back the legionary standards lost by Crassus, and Parthia (briefly) recognized Armenia as Rome's client, a diplomatic success that propagandists cried up as a great Roman victory. But the four legions Augustus stationed in Syria, to control that wealthy province and protect the eastern frontier, posed little threat to Parthia, as it realized. The kingdom of Armenia, a pivotal buffer or sometimes client state, caused more problems as it wavered between Rome and Parthia. Nero's fine general Corbulo, by mixed diplomacy and arms, arranged a Roman investiture (crowning) for an Arsacid (Parthian) king of Armenia in AD66, so appeasing both sides.

The Flavians had advanced the frontier east by annexing small client states. Trajan continued this policy, peacefully annexing Arabia Petraea (Jordan) in AD106 with its rich trading city of Petra, and building a military highway through the desert, so rounding off the eastern frontier. Although Antioch, the empire's third largest city, was only 100 miles (160km) from the frontier, the Parthians remained a minor threat. Trajan did not need to launch a war of conquest, but it seems he felt drawn east. Using Parthian interference in Armenia as an excuse, he launched a grand attack on the Parthians from the headquarters he set up at Antioch in late AD113.

Left: Trajan's conquest of the east started with a successful attack on Armenia in AD114. A massive assault then over-ran all Mesopotamia down to the Gulf. But the Romans' rapid advance left their flanks exposed to counter-attacks while Jewish revolts in the rear threatened Rome's hold of the east. Finally, Trajan's failure to take the key city of Hatra led to the collapse of the invasion even before his death in AD117.

Below: Trajan shown triumphant in military uniform, a captive crouching at the feet of this most genial but expansionist of emperors.

RETREAT FROM THE GULF

Armenia was annexed in AD114 and at first the conquest of Mesopotamia seemed a huge success. Ctesiphon fell and Trajan sat on the Golden Throne of the Parthian kings, hailed by his army as *Parthicus* (conqueror of Parthia). East of the Tigris, a new province of Assyria (approximately Kurdistan) was created, completing the project of detaching what is now Iraq from Iran, and Trajan sailed south down the Tigris to the Gulf. According to Cassius Dio, on seeing the ocean and a ship setting out for India he said, "I would certainly have gone there too had I been younger." But he was 65 and in poor health. He returned via Babylon, already a ruin, to see the room where Alexander had died 400 years earlier. There he received news that all his new conquests were in peril. A wave of Jewish revolts had broken out, while the Parthians were harrying the eastern flanks of the new provinces. Failing to take the city of Hatra in central Mesopotamia, Trajan began recalling his troops. He died of a stroke in AD117 in Cilicia, but his eastern conquests had pre-deceased him. Hadrian completed the withdrawal and the return to the status quo, except that Armenia was once more in the Roman sphere.

Later campaigns in the reign of Marcus Aurelius between AD162 and 166 were scarcely more successful. Although Seleucia was captured and destroyed, a devastating plague sprang from its ruins. It was left to Septimius Severus to establish a defensible new frontier in AD198 along the lines of the Khabur river and Jebel Singara ridge, making northern Mesopotamia a defensible bulwark. But his victory also proved costly in the longer run, for it so weakened the Parthian empire that it was replaced 30 years later by the far more aggressive Sassanids.

CHAPTER V

DEFENDING THE EMPIRE

After Trajan's death amid the ruins of his plans for conquering Asia, Hadrian reverted to a generally defensive policy. This was on the whole continued by his successors, despite later minor offensives. A few of these proved successful, like Septimius Severus' annexation of upper Mesopotamia, but most, like Marcus Aurelius' wars on the Danube or Septimius' own Caledonian campaign, failed with the death of their imperial instigator.

A total and official lack of aggressive wars, which had long kept soldiers busy and offered them chances of booty and promotion, posed its own problems. Hadrian addressed these by conducting vigorous exercises, which kept troops on their mettle, and by a huge fortifications programme, of which Hadrian's wall across northern England is only the most famous example. These walls were mostly built by legionaries themselves, so fulfilling the double function of adding to the empire's security while keeping its defenders occupied. But with some 6,000 miles (c.9,600 km) of land frontier, even Rome could not wall them all, and natural frontiers had to be exploited whenever possible. In the shorter term these proved adequate to protect the empire from its external foes, provided that no civil wars distracted the troops, especially when fortifications were supported by colonies of veterans. But certain corners of the empire always posed special problems, which drove even Hadrian to aggressive wars.

Left: Ruins of a milecastle on Hadrian's Wall, England, the most impressively surviving fortified frontier in the empire.

THE DILEMMAS OF DEFENCE

Above: Imperial policy moved decisively on to the defensive under Hadrian, but there was no change in military tactics.

Below: The cardo maximus (High Street) of ancient Gerasa (Jerash), Jordan, one of the many cities that thrived in the 2nd century AD.

For a long time, the Roman empire famously lacked a proper central reserve. The 25 legions Augustus left at his death in AD14 were deliberately dispersed on distant frontiers after inner provinces such as Spain were pacified. They were supplemented by equal numbers of cheaper auxiliaries. The only central force the *princeps* had at his command were the nine Praetorian cohorts, stationed in Italy and in Rome itself. These were crack troops but too few in number (*c*.4,500) to form more than a large bodyguard.

Some military historians have condemned Augustus' policy as a short-sighted economy that left the empire vulnerable to any invasion once the thin perimeter defences of legionary and auxiliary forts had been pierced. Others have condoned it as springing from the Principate's limited finances and the resultingly skimpy army, which had to defend nearly 4,000 miles (6,400km) of frontier with only 300,000 men. Both have argued over the dilemmas of defence: whether it should be preclusive, making invasion impossible by investing all manpower in a heavily fortified border, or whether it should be a defence in depth. This would rely on a massed central reserve swinging into action against intruders but would leave outer provinces exposed as "marcher" territories. The fate of the later empire, however, which had a strong central reserve and also many troops on the perimeter, yet which was finally overwhelmed, suggests that such arguments miss the point.

There was little purpose in having a strong central force stationed at Milan so long as the main power of the army was its heavy infantry, as it was until the late 3rd century AD. Legions with baggage trains could not march more than 15 miles (24km) a day even on Rome's fine roads. Cologne on the Rhine was 67 marching days from Rome, for example, while the journey from Rome to Antioch took 124 days hard marching.

Nor could Romans make much use of marine internal lines of communications. At the heart of the empire, the Mediterranean scarcely offered speedy alternative transport, and the Roman army avoided sea travel wherever possible as it was too risky. The sea could be too rough for travel even within the normal sailing season of April to October, as ancient navigation skills were limited. It could take 55 days to reach Syria by sea – faster than by land but still slow. Logistics argued against a large central reserve, which could not reach a threatened area in time. Instead, troops were withdrawn from one currently peaceful front to fight on another troubled one. This could cause problems – one reason Agricola could not complete his conquest of northern Britain was because Domitian had recalled some of his troops to fight the Dacians – but

ATLANTIC OCEAN

Colonia Agrippina

Colonia Agrippina-Rome
67 days marching time

Ostia-Massilia
3-10 days
Aquileia
Massilia

Ostia-Tarraco
Minimum 5 days
Tarraco

Rome
Ostia

Dyrrhachium

Ostia-Carthage
3-5 days by sea

Carthage

Panticapaeum

BLACK SEA

Chalcedon

Rome-Antioch
124 days (+2 days at sea)

Antioch

Rhodes

M E D I T E R R A N E A N

Apollonia

Alexandria
Rhodes-Alexandria
4 days

Left: Rome's almost central position in the Mediterranean did not help its military communications as much as might be expected. Moving troops from one frontier to another, whether by land or sea, was generally a slow business – one reason why emperors long dispensed with a central reserve that could not have reached threatened areas in time.

fortunately not more than one frontier was seriously threatened at any one time before the 3rd century AD.

However, the legions of the earlier Principate were *not* usually stationed to hold a fixed perimeter, although auxiliaries might patrol one. Legions were stationed in often indefensible spots so that they could pre-empt, or react to, any attacks before invaders had harmed unprotected lands behind the frontiers. One of Rome's boasts about the *Pax Romana* (Roman peace) was that its citizens had no more need of arms when only a few miles from the frontier than they did in Rome itself. There were, moreover, cogent political reasons for not having a large reserve force, especially one stationed in Italy. Armies were long commanded by legates of senatorial standing – potential rivals for the imperial throne as numerous revolts distracting emperors, from Saturninus in AD89 to Avidius Cassius in AD175, showed. Even without ambitious generals, after the Year of the Four Emperors in AD68–9 the armies grew conscious of their king-making potential. From the 3rd century AD onwards, the soldiers hailed their commanders as emperors with catastrophic frequency.

RESERVE OR BODYGUARD?

Septimius Severus, victor of the civil wars of AD193–7, purged the Praetorian guard, replacing them with his soldiers and stationing a newly created legion, the Second Parthica, near Rome. This created a force of 15,000 men, anticipating a central reserve. In the AD260s, Gallienus created a new reserve at Milan, using mostly cavalry *vexillationes* (detachments) from many legions. By the time this force was established, Gallienus had lost control of much of the empire, while the Danube frontier had collapsed and barbarians were threatening Italy. Milan therefore very nearly *was* the front line. It remained the main western capital after Roman recovery in the 4th century AD. By then, the Tetrarchy had begun a formal division between the *limitanei*, numerous frontier troops, and the *comitatenses*, superior mobile troops. Constantine took this further, concentrating the *comitatenses* and the new elite *palatini* in cities. The central reserve, 150,000 strong, had almost become a gigantic imperial bodyguard.

Below: Septimius Severus (AD193–211), under whom the empire reached its maximum permanent extent, began to create a central reserve by stationing a legion near Rome. But this, even when combined with the purged Praetorian guard, was still little more than a large imperial bodyguard.

NATURAL FRONTIERS
THE RHINE AND UPPER DANUBE

Above: If despotic and paranoid at home, Domitian (AD81–96) pursued a vigorous expansionist policy in south-west Germany.

The problems that faced all Roman imperial governments in the defences of the two key frontiers, the Rhine and Upper Danube, in the late 1st and 2nd centuries AD, derived from the geography of the region. Not long after it leaves Lake Constance, the river Rhine starts to make a reasonably good frontier. Fast-flowing, it soon enters a deep, almost gorge-like valley, navigable by the Roman patrol flotillas. By Mainz, it has become a formidable river and easily defended. But the Danube, most obviously in its early stretches before the Lech joins it, is not remotely such an effective water barrier.

Both rivers' upper reaches tended to freeze over in winter and shrink alarmingly in summer droughts, so making naval patrols often impossible and barbarian crossings all too easy. Even more worrying, the valley of the river Neckar offers enticing pathways up beyond the Danube's source for possible invaders. The land in the south-west corner of Germany is mountainous and well-wooded – the Black Forest still covers much of it today – and is therefore difficult to patrol. The obvious answer, which meant overturning Augustus' famous deathbed advice *"coercendi intra terminos imperii"* (keep within the frontiers of the empire), was to advance the frontier, to cut off the "re-entrant"

angle between the Rhine and Danube and also, incidentally, to shorten the overall frontier by about 170 miles (270km).

The Flavian emperors Vespasian, Titus and Domitian were the first to have the time, energy and perhaps the vision to attempt this. After the serious revolt by Civilis in AD69–70 in the lower Rhine, when many troops went over to the Gallic separatists, the entire Rhine frontier was systematically reorganized. Vespasian began splitting up the legionary camps to avoid concentrating too many soldiers under one general and rebuilding turf and timber fortifications in stone. He also ordered the annexation of the Black Forest, but left this frontier unsecured at its northern end. It was left to Domitian, the least loved of emperors to date (except perhaps by the army), to advance the frontier permanently and effectively.

Domitian's war of AD83–5 against the Chatti tribes, which was much ridiculed by Tacitus, led to the slow but systematic advancing of the frontier across the river Rhine to a line that exploited natural features, the steep rather than high Taunus Mountains and the river Main. This line linked up with Vespasian's Black Forest forts further south, pushing along the Neckar almost to the headwaters of the Danube, so cutting off half the re-entrant and projecting Roman power into central Germany. The land along the lower Main valley was very fertile, useful for feeding garrisons. Later, the Antonine emperors extended the *limes* – a term that had, by the 2nd century AD, come to mean a fortified line of defence, though originally it meant only a path or a boundary – to the Danube near Regensburg (Castra Regina), which was a legionary fortress. The road connecting the two rivers from Mainz to Regensburg became a major imperial highway, shortening the journey to the Danube by 11 vital days. By finally

Below: Hilly and thickly wooded, the Black Forest area remained impenetrable for the Romans until it was finally absorbed into the empire.

closing off this axis of potential invasion, this permitted the romanization of the areas far behind it. Although no real towns grew up within the new province, others lining the Rhine and Danube could now flourish in its shelter.

THE *AGRI DECUMATES*

This territory was known as the *Agri Decumates*, or lands that paid taxes, in contrast to "free Germany" beyond. A part of Upper Germany, the territory remained a militarized zone, but an increasingly prosperous one, defended by the longest and, in some ways, most imposing of all Roman fortifications. These were built mainly – initially entirely – of timber and turf, and included wooden watchtowers – probably with two men in them – every third of a mile (530m). These towers were easily visible to each other down lines cleared of woodland and linked by ditches. Palisades and even

hedges were added under Hadrian. The aim was not to interdict movement across the frontier completely – any more than with Hadrian's Wall – but to slow down and hamper any raiders and smugglers.

Auxiliary cohorts stationed every 5 miles (8km) or so backed them up, some of their forts being built in stone. In total, following the bends of rivers or the lines of hills in a way that makes sense on the ground if not on the map, the line covered some 300 miles (480km) with more than 60 forts and 900 signal towers. In fact this created a larger fortification than Hadrian's Wall, but, due to its mainly timber construction, it has left far fewer visible traces. (One or two forts, such as Zugmantel, have been reconstructed.) In the turmoil of the 3rd century AD, the line became increasingly difficult to hold and it was finally abandoned by AD260. The frontier then returned to its former limits under Augustus.

Above: South-west German reconstruction of a watchtower, typical of the hundreds that guarded the Agri Decumates.

Below: The Agri Decumates *reduced the length of the frontier and speeded communications.*

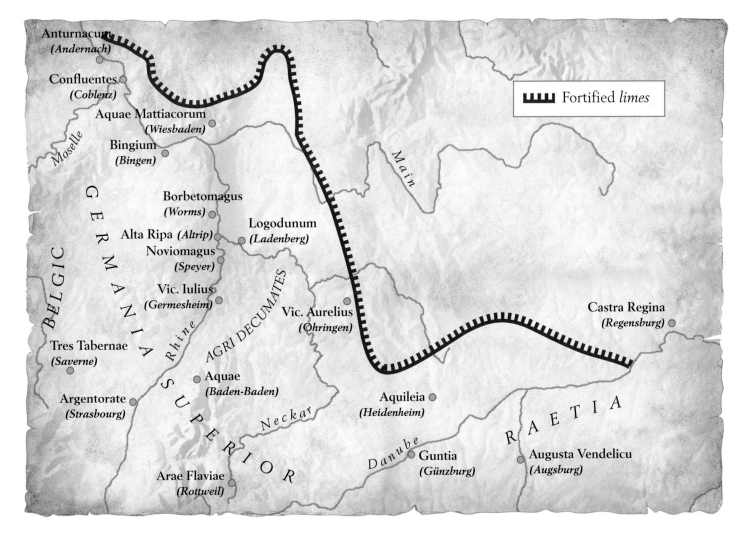

Fortified *limes*

Anturnacum
(Andernach)

Confluentes
(Coblenz)

Moselle

Aquae Mattiacorum
(Wiesbaden)

Bingium
(Bingen)

Main

G E R M A N I A

Borbetomagus
(Worms)

BELGIC

Alta Ripa (Altrip)
Noviomagus
(Speyer)

Logodunum
(Ladenberg)

Vic. Iulius
(Germesheim)

S U P E R I O R

Rhine

AGRI DECUMATES

Vic. Aurelius
(Öhringen)

Castra Regina
(Regensburg)

Tres Tabernae
(Saverne)

Aquae
(Baden-Baden)

Argentorate
(Strasbourg)

Neckar

Aquileia
(Heidenheim)

R A E T I A

Danube

Guntia
(Günzburg)

Augusta Vendelicu
(Augsburg)

Arae Flaviae
(Rottweil)

NATURAL FRONTIERS
THE MIDDLE AND LOWER DANUBE

Above: This scene from Trajan's Column in Rome shows Roman soldiers cutting down trees to build fortifications or war machines during the Dacian wars. At times, the army's demands could deforest whole regions.

Augustus had given Rome its longest land frontier – along Europe's longest river – when he occupied all the Danubian lands from the Alps down to the Black Sea. This was for a long time the empire's least developed region. It lacked any real towns or even the rich, if still predominantly agricultural, culture of pre-Roman Gaul and Britain. It was strategically important, however, because it dominated Italy's most accessible passes through the Julian Alps and provided a land route from the eastern empire to the west.

Slowly, the area was organized into provinces. These ran behind the river from Alpine Raetia and Noricum (Switzerland, southern Bavaria/north Austria), through the plains of Pannonia with its large rivers – the Save and Drave as well as the Danube – to Moesia (Bulgaria and northern Serbia). Ultimately, the whole region was to become Rome's prime recruiting ground, providing many great later emperors including Aurelian and Constantine. It was a vital defence against invaders, as

they moved from deepest *barbaricum*, the barbarian world, to the empire. Its final loss foreshadowed the western empire's.

As on the Rhine, Augustus had not originally intended to halt his sweeping conquests on the south or west bank of the river. However, all plans to occupy part of Bohemia (so creating a new line along the Elbe down to the North Sea) had to be aborted after a major revolt in Pannonia and Dalmatia that started in AD6. Coupled with Varus' German disaster in AD9, this marked the end of Augustan expansionism, although the huge Danubian basin remained relatively lightly garrisoned. In the 1st century AD it had only six legions – two of them initially in Dalmatia rather than on the river – compared to the eight on the much shorter Rhine frontier.

Diplomacy (always a major part of Rome's defence), coupled with bribes, kept the various nomadic tribes and peoples of the Pannonian plain divided and harmless; the Iazyges were often paid to keep the menacing Dacians in check.

Right: Rome's long and potentially most dangerous frontier was the Danube, beyond which lay the immensity of the Eurasian steppes, source of endless new invasions. From the early 2nd century AD, this frontier required ever-larger garrisons. Once across its perimeter defences, barbarians could easily penetrate into Italy, as happened in AD166 and on many subsequent occasions.

Roman frontier
Provincial boundary

IUTHUNGI
Danube
RAETIA II
Lauriacum (Lorch)
Vindabona (Vienna)
NORICUM RIPENSE
Carnuntum (Petronell)
NORICUM MEDITERRANEUN
Lake Balaton
VALERIA
Aquincum (Budapest)
PANNONIA I
Drava
VENETIA & HISTRIA
Aquilea (Grado)
Tergeste (Trieste)
SAVIA
Mures
Olt
PANNONIA II
Viminacium (Kostaloc)
Sirmium (Mitrovica)
DACIANS
Danube
SCYTHIA
DALMATIA
MOESIA I
A D R I A T I C   S E A
DACIA
MOESIA II
DACIA RIPENSIS
THRACIA
BLACK SEA
PRAEVALITANA
DARDANIA
HAEMIMONTUS
Philippopolis (Felibe)
Adrianople (Edirne)

Right: Marcus Aurelius (AD161–80) whose trans-Danubian plans expired with him.

However, when Decebalus, a formidable ruler, became High King of Dacia in *c.*AD85, his country's potential was quickly mobilized. Heavy raids across the Danube into Pannonia generated a quick, if initially unsuccessful, Roman reaction. Domitian's wars with Dacia led to a truce that was more in Dacia's favour than Rome's, due to Saturninus' revolt in AD89. Domitian not only paid Decebalus a subsidy, which was common enough practice, but also lent him engineers to fortify his capital of Sarmizagetusa Regia, which was nothing of the sort. In the following years the Iazyges, a nomadic people, became a problem too, raiding across the Danube and requiring Rome's finally successful attentions. Trajan's great conquest of Dacia in AD101–6 needs, therefore, to be seen in the light of a breakdown of the whole earlier system. Its success can be gauged by the 60 years of prosperous peace that followed. Flotillas – one on either side of the Iron Gates Gorge, which divided the Danube – helped keep the river free of intruders, turning it into a useful waterway as much as an effective barrier.

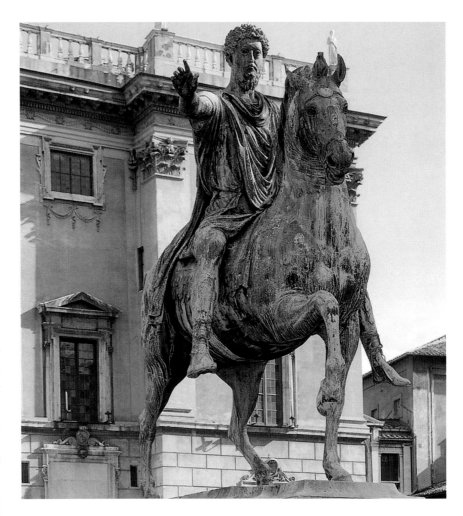

MARCUS AURELIUS'S CAMPAIGNS

The plague that devastated the empire from AD166 after the triumphant Parthian campaign (which itself had drawn off whole legions from the Rhine and Danube), gave the barbarians their chance. The Germanic Marcomanni and Quadi and the Iazyges crossed the lightly defended river and pushed on, bypassing forts, into Italy, attacking Aquileia (near Trieste) in AD167. For the first time in 260 years, barbarians were in Italy. Other barbarians opportunistically pushed through the Balkans to sack Eleusis, on the doorstep of Athens.

Marcus Aurelius, despite the plague and acute financial problems, raised two fresh legions (from gladiators among others), sold even the palace ornaments to pay for them and went north to repel the invaders. His long and hard campaigns along the Danube drove them back over the river. He now decided to copy Trajan, not out of vainglory – he was after all a philosopher – but from necessity. He probably intended to create new provinces of Marcomannia (the Czech Republic) and Sarmatia (Slovakia/Galicia). By advancing the frontiers, Rome would be able to meet the barbarian tide on the far side of the Carpathian and the Sudeten mountains. Whether his great project would have succeeded if the revolt of Avidius Cassius in Syria in AD175 had not distracted him and he himself had not died in AD180 is unclear. What is certain is that the Danube basin in the 3rd century became a key area for barbarian attacks. However, it had also become so deeply Romanized that it was a source of strength as well as weakness, right down to the fall of the western empire in the 5th century.

Below: A model of the key Dacian fortress of Bildaru in the mountains of Transylvania captured by Trajan's men.

NATURAL FRONTIERS
AFRICA, ARABIA, MESOPOTAMIA

Below: The ruins of the triple arch at Lambaesis (Tazoult, Algeria), built by Septimius Severus (AD193–211). The Libyan-born emperor was particularly interested in North Africa, embellishing its cities and advancing the frontiers.

Rome had desert frontiers in Arabia, Mesopotamia and North Africa. In Asia, Rome faced sporadic Arab raiders and its one equal, the Parthian, later Sassanid Persian, empire. In Africa, Rome often faced little – often no – opposition, for the deserts of Libya harboured only nugatory populations of Berber nomads. Egypt was almost impregnable behind its deserts, except from Asia, for upstream the Nubians – as Rome called the Sudanese – were no threat.

Cyrenaica and Tripolitania (Libya) may have needed almost no defence, but Roman Africa, that thin slice of the great continent seldom more than 100 miles (160km) deep, was an increasingly important province. Dry-farming employed a cunning combination of olive trees and wheat fields. It used every drop of moisture through irrigation and, by so holding back the desert, beneficially modified the climate. Africa satisfied much of Rome's demand for olive oil. Josephus described it as "that third part of the world, which feeds the city of Rome for eight months of the year and happily accepts taxation, although only one legion is stationed there".

For the Berbers it was worth raiding. To protect against their attacks, which generally followed the Atlas valleys as they ran down towards Carthage and its intensely fertile hinterland, a series of walls called *clausurae* (closures) were built. Some 15ft (4.5m) high, they closed off the valleys or at least made it extremely difficult for such invaders to return with

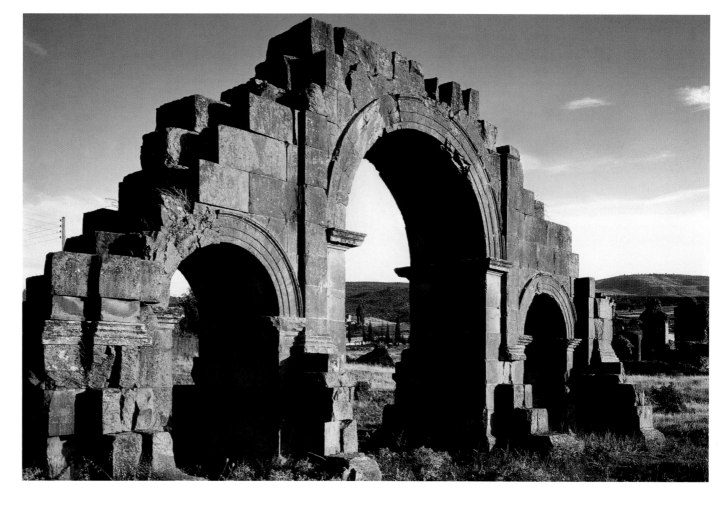

much booty. A joint letter from eastern and western emperors (Theodosius II and Honorius), written in AD409, indicates that Africa mattered to both parts of the empire. It also shows that there were *fossata* (ditch works) and *limites* (fortified lines) further south, where fertile land gives way to desert, with watchtowers.

Archaeology has tentatively confirmed this skeletal defence system, which exploited the *chotts* (sand seas, at times full of salt water) and mountains of the Haut Plateaux. Running from east to west, these were the *limes* of Tripoli, the *limes* of Numidia, inland from Carthage, and the *limes* of Mauretania, inland from the Algerian coast. None of these was a solid continuous defence like Hadrian's Wall, because the distances were too immense. Hadrian had ordered the construction of such a line on his visit to Africa in AD128. He realized that nomads and farmers were interdependent: nomads supplied useful extra seasonal labour, farmers repaid them with food-stuffs. The one legion was stationed at Lambaesis, just behind the central *limes*. Later, under Septimius Severus, forts were built much further inland. In Tripolitania Ghadames, some 300 miles (480km) inland, was the most advanced of four forts, built in AD200 and abandoned around AD263. Such forts were intended to control desert routes.

THE EASTERN FRONTIERS

Until Vespasian began annexing them, a screen of client states shielded the Roman provinces from the Arabian desert. But when Trajan took over Arabia Petraea (Jordan) in AD106, the problem of patrolling the edges of the Arabian desert confronted the Romans directly. Trajan built the Via Nova (new road), a military highway from the Gulf of Aqaba north-east past Bostra and Damascus. This was a patrolled *limes* in the old sense of a dividing line with forts built along it, from which cavalry patrolled. The Arabs were more numerous raiders than the Berbers – and in the 7th century AD became

invaders – but did not at this time pose a major threat to the blooming wheat fields of Transjordania. Later, Septimius pushed the frontier 50 miles (80km) east from the Via Nova, but it was further north that he made his major contribution, almost solving the perennial frontier problem with Parthia.

He did this by annexing upper Mesopotamia. Here his new frontier ran along the Khabur river, a small tributary joining the Euphrates 50 miles (80km) north of the key fortress of Dura-Europus, then running along the hills of Jebel Sinjar. These rise to 4,800ft (1,460m) above the desert – high enough to receive 8in (20cm) of rain a year, vital for supplying garrisons. Septimius probably stationed a legion at Singara on this line, and he certainly fortified Nisibis to its rear. His military road ran on to the Tigris at Eski Mosul (old Mosul). Here a walled city 3 miles (4.8km) in circumference was built, the easternmost limit of Rome's might. It would need a change of dynasty in Ctesiphon before such a powerful line would be challenged, and it lasted as long as the empire itself.

Above: The ruins of Dura-Europus on the Euphrates in Syria, once a vital fortress on Rome's eastern frontier. Captured by the Persians c.AD256 after a long siege, it was so badly damaged that it has never been reoccupied.

Below: These laws about the development of Roman lands in Africa are dated AD209.

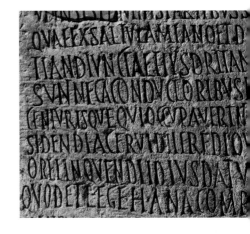

COLONIES AND SETTLEMENTS FOR VETERANS

Below: Colonies, originally planned chiefly for legionary veterans, were established right across the empire from the time of Julius Caesar onwards. They acted as a backup to regular legions and, more crucially if less intentionally, helped Romanize the empire. Colonies like York and Cologne later became important cities.

From the mid-Republic, Rome had expanded its power by the planting of colonies in strategically important places, first in peninsular Italy, then in Cisalpine Gaul. Originally, these *coloniae* were always settlements of Roman citizens with a standard Roman city constitution, but later some had only Latin rights, a halfway house to full citizenship that proved very useful in the Principate. All helped knit the empire together.

Gaius Gracchus had first proposed planting a colony for landless Romans outside Italy at Carthage, an idea revived by Saturninus in 102BC for the veterans of Marius' armies for North Africa, southern Gaul and Greece. However, it was Julius Caesar who started founding colonies for his veterans on a massive

scale: in Spain, where the charter of Urso (Colonia Genetiva Julia) survives and where older cities such as Cartagena and Tarragona became full Roman colonies; in Gaul, at Fréjus (Forum Julii) and Arles (Arelate); at Carthage and Corinth (both ruins since 146BC) and in Greece, Syria and even on the Black Sea coast. Many of these had strategic value.

Augustus, who reputedly had 300,000 veterans to find land for after Actium in 31BC, founded about 75 settlements. Twenty-eight were in Italy, such as Turin (Augusta Taurinorum), whose fine gate survives, and Aosta (Augusta Praetoria), facing the Alps. He stressed in the *Res Gestae*, his memoirs, that he paid fair prices for the land. More were scattered across the empire: Mérida and Zaragossa

(Caesar-Augusta) in Spain; Nîmes and Avignon in Gaul; Patras and Nicopolis (near Actium, "city of victory") in Greece; and on round the empire, in Africa, Macedonia, Syria, Galatia (north central Turkey) and Pisidia (central/south-west Turkey). Some were built for defence, such as those in Galatia and Pisidia, while others became thriving cities. Tarragona claimed to have a population of 400,000 in the 2nd century AD – which is probably an exaggeration, although it was the capital of the whole Iberian peninsula and a centre of the imperial cult.

All these generally small settlements – usually a couple of thousand veterans, growing perhaps into a city of between 10–15,000 – helped the urbanization and Romanization of the whole empire. Their elderly soldier-citizens could theoretically provide reinforcements to legionary forts and more certainly provided potential recruits for the next generation's legions. As they became permanent, some of the great military bases around the frontiers developed into towns with their outlying *canabae* (settlements). Sometimes, as at Cologne (Colonia Agrippina) in AD51, a colony was founded on the Rhine's west bank to incorporate these. In eastern Algeria, a Trajanic veterans' colony at Timgad (Thamugadi), has remained almost perfectly preserved, its porticoes and arches looking out over a now desiccated but once very fertile landscape.

PROUD TO BE ROMAN

As the colonies became established, they developed a competitive pride in being Roman. Local aristocracies, especially in the west – the long-Hellenized east was rather different – vied to become Roman in clothes, deed and name. Men whose fathers had been Gaulish chieftains began taking Roman triple names and their sons began to think of themselves as Romans. In Vienne (Vienna) on the banks of the Rhône, for example, Strabo reported early in the 1st century AD that "the Allobroges used to be always at war but now they

farm the plains and valleys, living in villages except for their nobles who live in Vienne. That was once a village… but now they have made it into a city." Italians began settling there as early as 70BC, and a century later Claudius could praise it as *ornatissima et valentissima colonia* (an excellent, flourishing colony). Up river on the other side, its rival Lyons (Lugdunum, the "dun" recalling a Celtic origin) had a theatre for 11,000 spectators, an odeon for more select audiences seating 5,000 and a large, centrally heated basilica. Lyons prospered at the centre of Gaul's Roman road network.

Further north, the city of Trier (Augusta Treverorum) became a centre of industry and commerce where the tribe of the Treveri settled and became fully Romanized. A school of sculpture also developed there. The city later became the capital of Gaul, at times of all the west, with a basilica, baths and palaces. In Britain, the tiny but fully self-governing *colonia* of Gloucester (Glevum) was founded under emperor Nerva (AD96–8), joining Lincoln and Colchester in this prized status. More populous was nearby Cirencester (Corinium), which boasted the full range of civic amenities although it was not a *colonia*. Hadrian gave Latin rights to many settlements, whereby all members of their councils as well as their decurions (officials) received Roman citizenship. In this way, Roman civilization and citizenship were spread.

Above: The ruins of the theatre at Bostra, now in Syria, which thrived after Trajan annexed Arabia Petraea, making it the capital.

Below: An evening view of Timgad, Algeria, in what was then a very fertile province.

THE JEWISH REVOLT

Above: Perhaps the most holy of the religious treasures that the Romans brought back from their sack of the Temple in Jerusalem was the seven-branched candlestick, here shown on the Arch of Titus in Rome being paraded in triumph by soldiers.

Below: The bitter siege and total destruction of Jerusalem by Titus in AD70 led to the permanent ruin of the Temple restored by Herod, and so to the last stage in the Jewish Diaspora that had begun centuries earlier.

Uniquely among the disparate peoples of the empire, the Jews refused to accept the Graeco-Roman culture all around them, proudly aware that they had a tradition to rival it. The Romans, despite initial good intentions and a total lack of racist feeling, could not understand a people so different, in their exclusive monotheism, from any of their other subjects. Set between the wealthy provinces of Syria and Egypt, Judaea was too strategically important to be ignored, however. The Jewish Diaspora, which had started some three centuries before following the conquests of Alexander the Great, meant that Jews were already spread across the eastern part of the empire, and there was a Jewish community in Rome by Julius Caesar's time.

Herod the Great, who died in 4BC, had pursued a pro-Roman and Hellenizing policy. His kingdom came under direct Roman rule as a procuratorial province in AD6 because his less than competent successors quarrelled among themselves. Many of their Jewish subjects (Jews were not the only inhabitants of the kingdom, Hellenized Syrians being numerous) objected strongly to the house of Herod but did little, being divided: Samaritans versus Judaeans, reformist Pharisees against Sadducees, with the Zealots as politically active extremists. However, when Rome gradually found itself ruling almost the whole area after the death of Herod Agrippa II in AD44, Jewish resentment was unified against the hated occupier. The troubled province of Judaea, one of the least popular posts for an equestrian governor, does seem to have been unusually badly administered.

A revolt finally broke out in AD66. It was centred on south Judaea and Jerusalem. The governor of Syria, Cestius Gallus, hastening south from Antioch with inadequate forces, was heavily defeated and beat a retreat. Encouraged by his defeat, other Jews now joined the revolt. The emperor Nero, who had become deeply suspicious of military rivals, entrusted the suppression of the revolt to Vespasian, an officer long out of favour but one who had had a good record of storming forts 20 years before in Britain. Vespasian proved a brilliant choice, methodically putting down the rebels, in particular reducing the fortress of Jotapata in Galilee under its Jewish commander, Josephus. By building a huge mound to approach its walls, the three legions involved were able to overwhelm the defenders, especially after Josephus changed sides. At this stage, however, Vespasian was distracted by the Civil War of AD68–9 and went to Alexandria to organize his empire-winning campaign. He left his son Titus to finish suppressing the Jews.

THE SIEGE OF JERUSALEM

By AD70, Titus had closed in on Jerusalem. Heavily fortified and ornamented by Herod the Great, the city was divided into five separately walled parts. It had been well provisioned, but fighting between rival groups of fanatics led to much of their food being burnt. Only at the very last minute did the Jewish factions cease fighting each other. The Old Upper City had Herod's huge palace on its west flank and just north-east of it lay the massively walled Temple Enclosure, with the Second Quarter and the larger New City to its north. Titus had four legions at his disposal, enough men to surround the whole city with a siege wall.

Although the defenders made aggressive sorties to attack the Romans, the final outcome was never in doubt. But at first the Romans' earthworks were undermined by the energetic defenders and collapsed. After rebuilding these and a further 13 days' fierce fighting, the Romans entered the less heavily defended New City and pushed on, breaking through the wall of the Second Quarter to attack the great fortress of Antonia (named after Mark Antony), which immediately adjoined the Temple. This required two new ramps. It fell only when the defenders' tunnels, meant to cause the collapse of these Roman works, actually

Below: The Arch of Titus, emperor AD79–81, was built to commemorate his victory in the Jewish war of ten years earlier.

undermined their own walls. A small group of legionaries then scaled the walls and killed the sentries, before sounding their trumpets to tell Titus to start the attack on the fort's inner walls. Weeks of heavy fighting were required to capture the Temple itself, which was burnt to the ground (perhaps accidentally). The loss of this great building, so central to Judaism, disheartened the defenders, but they fought on heroically. The Upper City was the very last to fall. After 18 days of preparation, during which legionaries and auxiliaries raised mounds on the west and east sides respectively, the Romans renewed their assault and finally stormed the area around the palace. The whole city was then pillaged before being systematically set on fire. During the five-month siege, the defenders had become so famished that, according to Josephus, mothers had eaten their own children. Titus ordered that just three towers and part of the wall be left, as poignant reminders of the ruined city.

Above: The siege and capture of Jerusalem in AD70 by the Romans under Titus was the crucial engagement of the Jewish revolt. The five-month siege saw the Romans circum-vallating the city as usual. They attacked the less well-defended New Town first, before moving upwards and inwards, firing the Temple and finally taking the Upper City, sparing no one in the city.

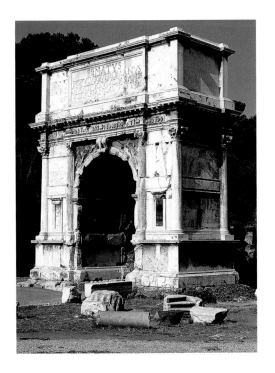

THE SIEGE OF MASADA

Above: An aerial view of one of the camps in the circumvallation at Masada, Israel, where several hundred Jewish zealots defied the Romans under Falvius Silva until AD73. Today, the desert site remains almost perfectly preserved due to its remoteness and aridity.

The last chapter in the bloody Jewish revolt of AD66–73 was the siege of Masada, which required one legion and 4,000 auxiliaries to suppress it. Famous because of its site, Masada is a rock rising some 1,300ft (396m) above a high, arid plateau, surrounded by precipitous cliffs that make it seem impregnable above the great valley of the Dead Sea. Herod the Great had converted it into a fortified palace and place of refuge, but by AD70 it was occupied by just a few hundred extremists, called the Sicarii. The fort was equipped with deep water cisterns and storerooms containing such vast amounts of food that it could not easily be starved out. Flavius Silva, legate of the Tenth Legion, therefore decided on a direct assault. This would make a dramatic statement about Rome's power and the perils of challenging it. It has left the most graphic and complete evidence of Roman siege warfare of any site.

The legionaries built a wall of local stone some 4,700yd (4,300m) long with towers every 30yd (27m) or so to circumvallate the rock, plus eight forts

for themselves, inside which they built low-walled cabins. Across the tops of these they put their leather tents, for protection against the blazing midday sun and the bitterly cold night winds of the three-year siege. They then built a huge ramp up the west side of the hill and winched their siege engines up it. Realizing that they could not escape, the Sicarii men committed mass suicide, after killing all their women and children. This finally ended the revolt – at least according to Josephus, the rebel leader turned Roman, who was, however, not an impartial observer.

BAR KOCHBA'S REBELLION

The fall of Masada did not, however, end simmering Jewish discontent with Roman rule across the eastern Mediterranean. Even before Trajan's grand attack on the Parthian empire faltered in AD117, a huge Jewish revolt in Cyrenaica, Cyprus and Egypt had flared up in AD115. More than 200,000 Greek-speaking neighbours of the Jews in these countries were reportedly

Right: The fortress–palace built by Herod the Great on the northern side of Masada as a place of refuge in case his subjects ever turned against him. Herod never needed it, but his fortifications helped the Sicarii defy Rome until the very end of the Jewish revolt.

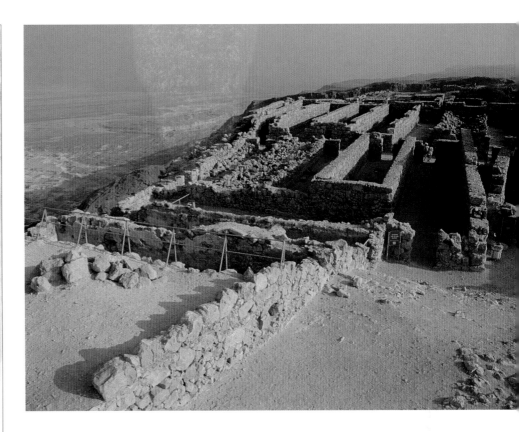

ROME AND THE JEWS

Looking at Rome's repeated suppression of Jewish revolts, we might imagine that the Romans were deeply anti-Semitic. Nothing could be less true. As the cases of Herod Agrippa, a close friend of the emperor Claudius, St Paul – a Jewish Roman citizen – and especially of Flavius Josephus demonstrate, the Romans were not racist in any modern sense. Nor were they religiously intolerant like many later Christian persecutors of Jews. In general, the Romans were indifferent to racial and religious differences, despite having a certain distaste for unwashed, drunken Germans. Their crushings of Jewish rebellions were always politically motivated, carried out with their usual brutality so as to discourage others.

The Romans first encountered the Jews in the mid-2nd century BC. They had just revolted against the Seleucid Hellenistic monarchs of Syria, who had tried to enforce the cult of Zeus (Jupiter) at Jerusalem. Out of distrust for the Seleucids, Rome supported this Maccabean revolt and Judaea became independent with Roman approval. The Romans were at first impressed, if puzzled, by the conservatism of Jewish religious beliefs and social customs, and they tried to accommodate them. Jews were generally exempted from emperor worship – such worship was a political rather than religious act – and military service was seldom forced on Jews for the same reason. A few Romans, attracted by its highly ethical message, converted to Judaism in the 1st century AD before the spread of Christianity. However, Jews were by then scattered so widely across the empire – in Syria, Egypt, Asia Minor (Turkey), Cyrenaica (Libya), Cyprus and even Rome itself – that Rome was inevitably drawn into many local Jewish–Gentile quarrels.

killed before the Romans managed to repress it. Yet this was still not quite the end of the Jewish–Roman wars.

Hadrian was among Rome's wisest and most humane emperors. He probably envisaged the empire becoming an equal commonwealth of all its provinces rather than being ruled just for Rome's sake. However, as a passionate philhellene (lover of Greece), he did not understand why any people should not want to participate in the splendours of Graeco-Roman culture. He therefore established a Roman colony at Jerusalem, which he renamed Aelia Capitolina, building a temple to Zeus/Jupiter on the very site of the ruined Temple. This so enraged the Jews still living in Palestine that in AD133 they rose again under Bar Kochba, a talented general, and proclaimed their own state. It took the Romans years of bitter, small-scale fighting to suppress this revolt, after which Jews were banned from Jerusalem. Later, Antoninus Pius (reigned AD138–61) quietly revoked his predecessor's decree and gave any Jews who wished it permission to return to the now utterly desolate site of Jerusalem.

Above: Storehouses and deep wells inside the fort of Masada. It was so well supplied that the Romans could not hope to starve it quickly into surrender.

Below: Remains of the Jewish fortification at Masada. Behind its walls, Zealots called the Sicarii retreated, thinking they had made themselves impregnable to all attacks.

CHAPTER VI

DECLINE AND FALL

Few historical topics are more fascinating than the decline and fall of world-conquering powers. In Rome's case this took centuries rather than years. The empire had survived a near-total collapse in the 3rd century AD and even the 5th century AD saw only the fall of the western half of the empire – and half of that was recovered by the eastern empire in the 6th century AD. The story is much more complicated than one of inexorable decay.

Although there were a handful of brilliant or exceptional barbarian leaders, notably Attila the Hun and Gaiseric the Vandal, most of the barbarians who overran the empire in the 5th century AD were not especially formidable. Similar tribes had already tried to invade the empire in the preceding centuries and been repulsed, albeit at an often huge cost. This suggests that the fall of the western half of the empire might have been averted by intelligent, consistent and, above all, unified strong government. But the imperial rulers' record in the 5th century AD is one of indecision, feebleness and above all of suicidal disputes, as internecine fighting squandered Rome's remaining strength in civil wars. It was hardly surprising that some, although never all, of the brightest and the best citizens of the western half of the Roman world finally lost faith and hope in their government, turning instead to the City of God to be found only in heaven.

Left: Sacrificing to the pagan gods – a political as well as religious gesture that vexed an increasingly Christian empire.

THE 3RD-CENTURY CRISIS

Above: The reign of the perverted emperor Elagabalus drew Rome further into her 3rd-century AD crisis.

Below: The Emperor Decius addresses his troops. He became the first Roman emperor to be killed (by the Goths) in battle in AD251, setting an ominous precedent.

In some ways it is remarkable that the Roman Empire survived the 3rd century AD at all. The civil wars, foreign invasions, plagues and other calamities it suffered for more than half a century after 235AD would have been enough to cause the terminal disintegration of most empires. But centripetal patriotism, a loyalty to the idea as much as to the reality of Rome, proved in the end just strong enough to ensure the empire's survival, for a while. It survived, however, in a different form and at a price that grew steadily more crushing, financially, socially and politically.

Cracks in the golden surface of the *Pax Romana*, the Roman peace, had appeared as early as the reign of Marcus Aurelius (AD161–80). The plague – possibly smallpox – which the victorious legions brought back with them from Parthia in AD165, devastated the empire and kept recurring for years. Combined with a series of invasions, primarily but not exclusively along the Danubian frontier – even Egypt suffered a brief attack – followed by the long debauchery of Commodus' reign, this epidemic hit an already somewhat sclerotic empire. The empire's economy had almost certainly started to stagnate by the mid-2nd century AD; by the century's end it was probably contracting.

Far worse, however, were the civil wars that followed Commodus' assassination in AD192. Septimius Severus finally won the civil wars in AD197 but at a terrible cost, both military and economic. Both Severus' and his enemy Albinus' armies had huge casualties in the last campaign. In these wars, trained Roman soldiers were killed fighting each other, a loss the empire could no longer easily make up. Severus, a brutally vindictive man, sacked Lugdunum (Lyons) so thoroughly it never recovered its wealth or status as Gaul's prime city. By comparison with his thuggish son Caracalla, he was an ideal ruler, but the latter's murder brought no improvement for there followed the reign of the manic pervert Elagabalus.

The murder of the last Severan, the ineffectual Alexander, in AD235, is usually taken to mark the end of the Principate and its replacement by mere anarchy. The year AD238 saw the coinage of seven distinct emperors and there were at least 50 claimants to the imperial throne in the half century after AD235. Some of these formed wholly separate states, such as the Gallic, British and Spanish empire of Postumus.

The problem of the succession, always tricky in the crypto-monarchy that was the Principate, became crucial in the ensuing chaos. Of the 27 or so "regular" emperors, 17 were killed by their own troops or officers, two were forced to commit suicide, one died a natural death and the rest were killed in battle. Even outstandingly successful and popular emperors such as Aurelian (AD270–75) were murdered. The custom by which the Senate had sanctioned (even if it did not always control) the choice of the next emperor became an outmoded farce. Elevation to the imperial purple became effectively a deferred death sentence.

The barbarian peoples outside the empire had long been waiting for an opportunity to renew their raids. Now, with the Romans at each other's throats, they saw and seized it. Tarragona and Athens, both many hundreds of miles from a frontier, were sacked in the AD260s. Once barbarians had penetrated the outer frontier defences, Rome's good roads facilitated their raids, now that there were no longer forces waiting to repel them. The interior cities, with their long-disarmed citizens and no tradition of self-defence, were easy prey. Soldiers had to be called in to build many of the walls for the cities in Gaul, for example.

ECONOMIC CRISIS

This damage to life across the provinces far beyond the traditional frontier zones proved hard to repair. At the same time the increase in the size and cost of the army meant a steep rise in taxes. Septimius Severus had increased Rome's military strength to 400,000 men and raised the army's pay by 50 per cent – perhaps an overdue rise, but Caracalla raised their pay again by another 50 per cent. To pay

for this and subsequent increases, Caracalla debased the coinage, a custom followed by so many of his successors that money became almost worthless. By the mid-3rd century AD, many traders and bankers were refusing to accept Roman coins. The armies resorted to exacting goods and services from the unfortunate civilians they were supposedly protecting.

The economic results were grim but are unquantifiable, for it was an economically ignorant age. It is estimated that at least 15 per cent of all arable land went out of production in the mid-3rd century AD. (Egypt, however, was probably thriving, and archaeological evidence from North Africa also suggests a period of economic prosperity.) But city life, especially in the west, also suffered terribly. The walls Aurelian gave Rome covered most of its existing urban area, but other cities shrank drastically. Within them, the old decurion class of local officials, who had been in many ways the backbone of the empire, began to collapse beneath an increasing burden of taxes. Those rich enough to do so withdrew to self-sufficient country estates; the less wealthy sank back into the urban poor. No matter what the tetrarchs and their heirs attempted, the blow to civic life, especially in the west, was to prove irreparable.

Above: Relatively unharmed by the 3rd-century crisis, North Africa still prospered, building amphitheatres such as this at El Djem, Tunisia.

Below: Philip the Arab (AD244–9) was the emperor who celebrated Rome's millennium in AD248, but it was not a timely celebration. The empire appeared to be collapsing. Barbarians had broken through on almost every frontier, while anarchy spread inside the empire.

THE EASTERN PROBLEM
THE POWER OF THE SASSANIDS

Above: The power of the Sassanids of Persia lay in their cavalry. This cataphract (armoured horseman) charging with his lance formed the backbone of the army, although their lack of stirrups limited their impact.

Below: This citadel, called the Redoubt, overlooks the river Euphrates in Syria at Dura-Europus on the two empires' much-disputed frontier. Both the Romans and the Persians appear to have occupied this citadel at different times.

For nearly two and a half centuries after the battle of Actium, Rome could regard the defence of its eastern frontier along the mid-Euphrates as something of an optional extra. The Arsacid Parthian empire facing it across the upper Euphrates may have been very large (it covered modern Iraq, Iran and parts of south Afghanistan), but it was seldom formidable, except when on the defensive. The Parthian empire's loose semi-feudal structure meant that its sub-kings did not always rally to help their nominal overlord.

Despite this, the Parthians had repelled Roman invaders from Crassus to Trajan, but they never seriously threatened Syria, the Roman province closest to them. Septimius Severus' campaigns in the AD190s again showed up Parthian weakness – he sacked Ctesiphon and annexed upper Mesopotamia, establishing a very defensible frontier province. However, he also unwittingly damaged the prestige of the Arsacid dynasty so badly that it succumbed to Ardashir, a Sassanid prince, in AD224.

The Sassanids came from the province of Persis (Fars). Guardians of Persepolis, Iran's ancient royal city, they were determined to revive the glories of the Achaemenid Persian empire of Darius and Xerxes. This had once extended west as far as the Aegean, so major conflict with Rome seemed inevitable. Early clashes were inconclusive, however. Neither Alexander Severus nor Gordian III were good generals, but their armies, ably officered, managed to avoid defeat, at least according to Roman sources.

The Sassanid army consisted of heavy cavalry – cataphracts, mainly noblemen and their supporters, who charged using lances – supplemented by numerous mounted archers. The Romans commented admiringly on the disciplined skill of these archers, which rivalled that of the legionaries' and was well suited to desert terrain. Persian infantry was of little use, but the Sassanids at times employed Indian elephants to great psychological, if not military, effect. Above all, the Sassanids developed a professional siege corps, something the Parthians had lacked but which was essential for attacking the walled cities of Mesopotamia and Syria. The Sassanids also revived the old Zoroastrian religion, a form of monotheism that stressed martial values and gave their empire a strong ideological basis.

In AD241 Shapur I succeeded to the throne (the Sassanids generally followed the hereditary principle) and began calling himself "King of Kings of Iran and non-Iran", a universalist title to challenge that of Rome. His reign of 32 years outlasted those of 16 Roman emperors. His western offensives began with forcing the new emperor, Philip the Arab, to make a humiliating peace in AD244. His second offensive in AD256 ended with the capture of 37 Roman cities,

Above: The "Arch of Chosroes" stands in the ruins of the audience hall of the Sassanian palace of Ctesiphon, near Baghdad, Iraq.

including Dura-Europus (which fell after an epic siege *c.*AD256) and Antioch, capital of the Roman east. All survivors were carried off into captivity. The emperor Valerian took a huge army of 70,000 men east to repel Shapur but it was hit by plague and cornered in Edessa. Valerian was captured and spent the rest of his life as a prisoner of the Persians, used as a human footstool by Shapur when the Persian king mounted his horse. After his death, Valerian's stuffed body was hung on the walls of a temple. The capture alive of a Roman emperor was an unprecedented humiliation for the empire but one that Gallienus, Valerian's son, was powerless to avenge.

The whole Roman east then seemed about to fall into Shapur's hands, as his forces overran Asia Minor and threatened Egypt. Fortunately for Rome, Shapur snubbed Odenathus, king of Palmyra, while returning to Persia in AD261. This proved a huge mistake. Odenathus accepted a Roman command. Palmyrene cavalry, perhaps the best in the east, now turned against Persia and Persian forces had to retreat for a time.

It would be a mistake to suppose that the Persians were always invincible. They had difficulty maintaining their conquests beyond the Euphrates so far from their Iranian power base. They could also be defeated in open battle, as Galerius, the Caesar of Diocletian, showed. After an initial defeat, Galerius triumphed over the Persian monarch, Narses, in AD298, annexing a useful slice of land beyond the Tigris. The subsequent peace lasted for 40 years.

JULIAN'S DEFEAT

Under Constantine and his successors, the peace unravelled. Constantius II spent much time in the AD340s fighting the Persians before turning west to deal with Roman rivals. The Persians then renewed the offensive, capturing the well-fortified city of Amida in AD359; they had been intending to bypass it until a catapult bolt killed the son of a client king and so forced them to attack. Julian, on becoming sole emperor in AD361, decided to avenge this defeat and crush Persia. After his defeat and death, half of Rome's territories east of the Euphrates were ceded to Persia by the new emperor Jovian in return for safe passage home. Oddly, the peace that followed lasted, with only minor disruptions, for 140 years.

Below: When the Sassanid Persian empire replaced the Parthians in c. AD226, Rome faced far greater pressure on its eastern frontier. The Persians penetrated deep into Roman territory in the 3rd century AD, but the Romans counter-attacked later, pushing across the upper Tigris. Julian's invasion of AD363, intended to finish off the Persians, ended in defeat with Rome having to cede half Roman (upper) Mesopotamia. From then on the frontier remained relatively stable.

FOREIGN INVASIONS
FRANKS, GOTHS, ALAMANNI, HUNS

Above: A Visigoth chieftain on horseback leading his men. Not all Visigoths were mounted, but their cavalry was more formidable than that of earlier German tribes.

Below: This sarcophagus from the 3rd century AD shows Romans and Germans fighting hand to hand. By this time, Rome's earlier superb military discipline could no longer automatically be relied upon to win the day.

For more than two centuries the Romans under the Principate had faced generally quite small barbarian tribes who, if at times fierce and tough fighters, were seldom any real match for Roman arms or diplomacy. The latter, along with judicious subsidies or bribes, generally kept most tribes divided against each other or within themselves.

However, centuries of living so close to a far more united and powerful state began to have an effect on the tribes inside Germany. By the 3rd century AD, the older, smaller tribes such as the Chatti and Cherusci had coalesced into two far more potentially threatening groups: the Alamanni in southern Germany, whose name means "all men", and the Franks on the lower Rhine, whose name means "free men". These were loose confederations of similar tribes, rather than unitary kingdoms, but they would combine for the specific purpose of attacking the Roman empire.

THE GOTHS

More formidable were other new peoples who emerged in the 3rd and 4th centuries AD, most notably the Goths. Probably originating in southern Sweden, they migrated slowly south-east (too far east for Rome's knowledge) into the southern Ukraine. The Goths finally burst upon the Roman world in AD245 when they crossed the Danube delta and raided Moesia. Soon they were pushing further south into Thrace (European Turkey and north-east Greece), and in AD251 the emperor Decius went to repel them. He was unsuccessful and became the first emperor to be killed in battle. Emboldened, the Goths renewed their raids over the next 17 years, at times even taking to the sea and ravaging the Mediterranean.

At this stage, most barbarians were after loot and plunder, not lands to occupy. The Goths were crushingly defeated by the emperor Gallienus, at the head of his new cavalry corps, at Nish in Serbia in AD268, losing 50,000 men. Subsequently, the Ostrogoth half of the federation – their name probably means east Goths – retreated to the Ukrainian steppes. There they became formidable horsemen, creating a kingdom stretching from the Don to the Vistula, while their Visigothic cousins established a smaller adjacent kingdom north of the Carpathians. Although it is now known that the Goths did not have stirrups, so useful for heavy horsemen, they were far more effective cavalry than any the Romans had hitherto faced in Europe and posed a threat of a new order. However, for the time being they seemed settled along the north of the Black Sea. The Vandals were a Germanic tribe similar to the Goths, fewer in number but, it later turned out, even more opportunistic under the right leader.

Left: From the mid-3rd century AD on, Rome found itself facing new, much more formidable, groups of barbarian invaders than earlier. Some, such as the Franks and Alamanni in Germany, were coalitions of older tribes, but others, such as the Goths, were totally new peoples. These invaders penetrated frontier defences depleted by Roman civil wars to reach and sack cities as far afield as Tarragona in the west or Athens in the east. The emperor Gallienus' seemingly crushing defeat of the Goths at Nish in AD268 merely checked the invasions.

CHRISTIAN BARBARIANS

A new factor by the late 4th century was that some German peoples – the Visigoths, Ostrogoths and Vandals – had converted to Christianity. Unfortunately for them, it was not orthodox Catholic Christianity but Arianism, a heretical school that denied the divinity of Christ and followed the teachings of Arius, a Libyan cleric. Far from creating a tie with an increasingly Christian Roman empire, their Arianism served to separate Germans, as the one thing worse than a pagan to the Roman Church was a heretic.

One reason why the Franks became the ultimate victors in Gaul, giving their name to the new country, was that Clovis, their first great king, converted to Catholicism in AD496, so making his people acceptable to his Gallo-Roman subjects. Clovis married Clotilda, a Burgundian princess. The Burgundians, too, chose Catholicism and so became permanently embedded in their corner of Gaul, while the Visigoths, Ostrogoths and Vandals, despite conquering Spain, Italy and North Africa respectively in the 5th century, have vanished like smoke.

All the Teutonic invaders, no matter how uncouth and evil-smelling to the Romans, were nothing in comparison to a totally new threat from Asia that emerged in the late 4th century AD. The Huns, originally known to the Chinese – who had built their Great Wall against precisely such terrors – as the Hsiung-nu, entered the outer orbit of the Roman world in about AD370. Ammianus, the great 4th-century historian, described them as, "the most savage and hideous of all races. They have short bull-like necks and their bodies are short and deformed … They are stuck to their saddles, eating, drinking, bartering, even sleeping wrapped round their horse's neck. In fighting they excel by the great speed of their attacks… They are brave in war, faithless at keeping truces, deceitful, quick to anger and insatiably greedy for gold." Directly and indirectly, these savage nomads played a crucial part in the destruction of the western empire, before they vanished from European history, leaving nothing but evil memories, and their name on the Hungarian plains, where they had briefly settled in the 5th century AD.

THE LOSS AND RECAPTURE OF THE EAST: AD260–72

Above: A triad of gods from Palmyra, the great trading city in the Syrian desert that came to Rome's help in the 3rd century AD and then tried to create its own empire before being crushed.

Below: The wealth and polyglot sophistication of Palmyra were reflected in its flamboyant architecture. Classically Graeco-Roman in form, this was often baroque in spirit, as this ruined monumental arch suggests.

Superbly sited in a large oasis between the great cities of Mesopotamia and the ports of Roman Syria, Palmyra had grown wealthy from the most lucrative trade in the ancient world: transporting silks, spices, precious stones and similar luxuries from India and China to Rome. Since the reign of Vespasian, or possibly even earlier, Palmyra had been a Roman dependency. Its exact status was uncertain but it clearly enjoyed enough autonomy to contribute separate cavalry forces to the Roman armies that Trajan and Septimius Severus led against Parthia.

The excellence of Palmyrene cavalry – which included heavy armoured cataphracts and light mounted archers, as well as some camels – seems to have originated from their long-established roles guarding the camel trains that crossed the desert against Arab raiders. The city had a Semitic, mostly Aramaic-speaking population, but its culture was a luxuriant mixture of Roman, Greek and Semitic. Palmyra's exuberantly decorated "baroque" temples and colonnades testify to its great wealth.

Such cultural links, as well as its geographical location on the west side of the Syrian desert, automatically inclined Palmyra to the Roman side in wars with Parthia or Persia. However, the catastrophic defeat and capture of the emperor Valerian in AD260, when all Rome's Asian provinces seemed about to fall into Persian hands, encouraged Septimius Odenathus, leader of the most powerful tribe of Palmyra, to consider changing sides. In AD261 he approached the Persian king Shapor and offered to join him. Shapor, flushed with victory after three successful wars against Rome, rejected the Palmyrene prince. This proved a colossal mistake. Impressive though the Persians' gains were, they were operating in hostile country and their supply lines were perilously extended across northern Mesopotamia and Syria, being particularly vulnerable to any attacks from the south. These attacks Odenathus now delivered.

Within a couple of years, Palmyrene cavalry had driven the Persians out of Syria and the Roman part of Mesopotamia. The emperor Gallienus, distracted by troubles far closer home, made Odenathus *Dux Orientis* (Governor of the East). Under this title, Odenathus became the effective ruler of almost all Syria. In AD266 he even advanced deep into the Persian empire and defeated the Persians outside Ctesiphon. In the following year he turned north and marched into northern Asia Minor to repel a Gothic attack. His domestic position was insecure, however, and he was murdered on his return from this campaign, possibly at the instigation of

Left: The essential frailty of Palmyrene power was revealed when the emperor Aurelian marched east and crushed the Palmyrene army in a series of battles, culminating in the capture of Palmyra itself. Queen Zenobia was also taken and her rich city sank into ruined obscurity.

Gallienus, who had grown alarmed at the extent of his victories. This was by no means, however, the end of Palmyrene power, for Odenathus' widow, Zenobia, at once took control of the new "empire".

CLEOPATRA'S DESCENDANT

Zenobia claimed descent from Cleopatra, the last Ptolemaic queen of Egypt and Mark Antony's doomed lover. She was certainly as beautiful (she was famed for her long black hair), and as ambitious, although she seems to have been a better military and diplomatic leader, winning over many Arab chieftains and princes to her cause. Palmyra, although a wealthy trading city, did not compare with the huge kingdom of Egypt, so Zenobia needed all the support she could find to continue her city's fine balancing act between the Roman and Persian giants.

Proclaiming herself regent to her young son Vaballathus, Zenobia reasserted Palmyrene control over Syria and Roman Mesopotamia, again winning the acquiescence of Gallienus and then of his successor Claudius II in AD268. However, when she invaded Egypt and Asia Minor in AD270, she openly broke with Rome. Alexandria held out against her and her forces were too thinly spread to control

most of the territories they had conquered. In AD272 she had Vaballathus crowned as *imperator* and Augustus, and she herself took the title of Augusta. Aurelian, the new emperor in Rome, would not accept this outright challenge and, after defeating the Goths again on the Danube, he marched east.

Although the Palmyrenes were still superior in cavalry, Aurelian managed to defeat them outside Antioch at Immae. In a second battle at Emesa, Zenobia was again defeated and retreated to Palmyra, hoping that Aurelian's army would be unable to supply itself in the desert. But it was Palmyra that ran short of food and Zenobia decided to escape and seek help from the Persians. Captured just as she was about to cross the Euphrates, she was taken back to Rome where she was paraded in gold chains in Aurelian's triumph the following year, before being allowed to retire to Tivoli. Aurelian spared Palmyra itself, possibly aware of its potential value as an ally, but news of a second revolt reached him in AD273. Quickly returning, he retook the city and punished its massacre of the small Roman garrison left there by sacking it so thoroughly that it soon passed almost completely out of history.

Above: Palmyra was typical in the way it absorbed the Hellenistic culture that had spread across Asia after Alexander and which Rome further encouraged.

THE SPLINTERING EMPIRE

Above: Gallienus, whose reign (253–68AD) saw the empire almost disintegrate.

Rome might have expected to find its conquests ever ready to revolt the moment that central power weakened. In AD68–9, the Year of the Four Emperors, there was indeed a serious rebellion. Civilis, a Batavian (from modern Holland) who was also a Roman citizen and commander of an auxiliary unit of Batavians, roused a revolt along the lower Rhine. He even persuaded some legions to join him before he was suppressed. Yet this was in fact almost the only significant revolt of its kind in Europe. From the time of the reign of Hadrian (AD117–38), the provinces were treated as equal partners in a commonwealth, a trend confirmed when Caracalla (chiefly for financial reasons) granted almost all free men Roman citizenship in AD212. When the empire nearly broke up in the 3rd century AD, it did so because Rome was not providing the protection the provinces expected and needed.

Gaul, the largest and probably most populous of the western provinces, was the leader in this revolt. There had long been a tendency by Rome to downgrade the importance of the Rhine frontier compared to the Danube. By the AD240s there were only four legions along the Rhine, as opposed to 12 on the, admittedly longer, Danube. The legions were also constantly weakened by calls for *vexillationes* (detachments), leaving too few troops to deal with the threat from the new confederacies: the Franks on the Lower Rhine and the Alamanni in southern Germany. Raids across the Rhine began in the AD230s, intensified in the AD250s and led to major invasions. The Franks penetrated through Gaul to sack Tarragona in north-east Spain in AD260, while the Alammani crossed the *Agri Decumates* and the Alps before being defeated near Milan in AD259. Then, in AD260, news of the emperor Valerian's humiliating defeat and capture by the Persians shook the Roman world to its very foundations.

In the circumstances, separatism appeared desirable. Marcus Postumus, a nobleman of Gallic descent and the governor of Lower Germany, was proclaimed emperor by his troops in AD260 after defeating some invaders. Marching on Cologne, he then captured and killed the emperor Gallienus' young son Saloninus, who had recently been made Augustus. Expelling barbarians and re-establishing the Rhine frontier, he won

Gallic Empire of Postumus 261
Gallic Empire of Tetricus 271

Left: The Gallic empire of Postumus included all Gaul, Britain and Spain. Tetricus ruled only part of Gaul and Britain.

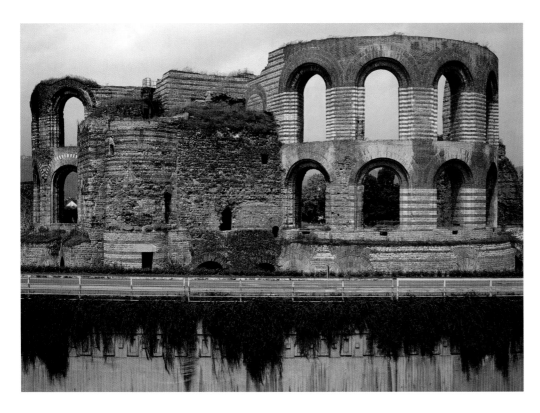

Left: The imperial baths of Trier, which probably date from the early 4th century AD. In the late 3rd century AD, the city became the proud capital of the separatist Gallic empire. Later it was the capital of the western Caesars under the Tetrarchy and throughout the 4th century.

recognition by the legions in Britain, Spain and even Raetia, so that the whole western quarter of the empire had seceded. Postumus made it clear that he did not intend to march on Rome, and was left in peace for five years. He then established a separate Senate at Trier, his capital, which he began fortifying and embellishing with an amphitheatre and palaces, while restoring the ravages made by barbarians. The Gallic empire seemed set to survive.

Gallienus recovered Raetia in AD263, but his attack on Postumus two years later in AD265 failed. Surviving Gallienus' murder by a year, Postumus was killed by his own troops in AD269 when he refused to let them sack Mainz after they had defeated another usurper. In the ensuing anarchy, Spain abandoned its Gallic allegiance, as did the south-east of Gaul, but the rest of that province and Britain remained independent until Aurelian led an army against them in AD274. The last Gallic emperor, Tetricus, seems to have reached some kind of understanding with Aurelian. Tetricus's life was spared and he even became governor of Lucania in southern Italy.

A BRITISH EMPIRE

Saxon raids along the coasts of Britain and northern Gaul had led to the expansion of the powerful *classis britannica*, the British fleet, which was based in large fortresses on each side of the Channel. Its admiral, Carausius, quarrelled with the western Augustus, Maximian, in AD286 – he was accused of pocketing Roman goods recovered from Saxon raiders – and declared himself independent. He was a skilful admiral and general, for he got the backing of his troops and maintained his hold on the Channel ports, defeating Maximian in AD289. Carausius then assumed the full panoply of titles, including Caesar, Augustus and *pontifex maximus* (chief priest), and on his coinage presented himself joint ruler with Diocletian and Maximian. Unimpressed, they sent Constantius Chlorus, the western Caesar, to defeat him. Constantius regained the Gallic ports, including Boulogne, in AD293. This led to Carausius' murder by his chamberlain Allectus, who took his place. Four years later, Constantius' invasion forces overwhelmed Allectus with a two-pronged attack and Britain was restored to the empire after ten years' independence.

Below: Roman soldiers from a Gallo-Roman carving. Gaul became so deeply Romanized that the separatist empire of Postumus copied Rome's, complete with Senate and baths. But Gaul returned to the empire by AD274.

THE FIRST RECOVERY
AD260-76

Above: The Porto San Sebastiano, one of the heavily fortified gates in the Aurelianic walls around Rome, was extended by Valentinian I and Honorius.

Below: The largest and most imposing walls in the 3rd century AD very suitably encircled the capital. Built by the emperor Aurelian, they proved effective against direct assault but not blockades.

By AD260, in the wake of the capture of the emperor Valerian by the Persians and the loss of his huge army, the empire seemed doomed to disintegration. Decades of civil wars had alerted the barbarians to its weaknesses, and invasion followed invasion: the Alamanni had finally overrun the *Agri Decumates* by AD260 and threatened southern Gaul and northern Italy; the Franks crossed the Lower Rhine and soon reached Spain; the Goths, Heruli and Gepids poured through Dacia and into Moesia, sacking cities as far apart as Trebizond in AD255 (north-east Turkey) and Athens in AD267, while Saxons raided the coasts of Britain and a German tribe, the Juthungi, ravaged central Italy. On top of all this, the empire had been suffering from plague intermittently for years. The economy, already stagnant if not in decline earlier in the century, now declined still faster, although some untouched areas such as Egypt and North Africa seem to have remained quietly prosperous. Everywhere

rapid inflation continued, fuelled by successive tamperings with the coinage that gave the government a short-term boost at a crippling long-term cost.

For the first time in centuries, men began openly to despair of the power of the Romans, looking around for alternatives, be they manifestly separatist emperors in Gaul or effectively independent Palmyrene rulers in the east. Yet amazingly, at this darkest hour, a recovery began that within two decades had stabilized most of the frontiers, expelled most of the barbarians and even begun to reform the army, currency and administration. The credit for beginning this turnaround must go to the emperor under whom the empire had seemed lost and who has long been maligned for it: Gallienus.

Gallienus had been co-emperor with his father since AD253, being left in command of the west while Valerian went east in AD254. He had a major success in turning back the Juthungi in

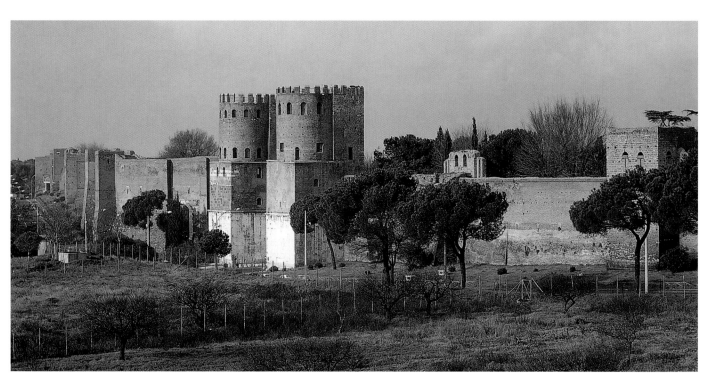

AD259 from their first Italian attack, but the news of his father's defeat triggered a rash of usurpers; traditionally, 20 pretenders arose in his reign. They forced him to spend as much time fighting rivals as barbarians, although he temporarily acknowledged the independence of the Gallic empire under Postumus in AD260. He did so to concentrate on the defence of Italy, where he made Milan his effective capital. Here he assembled a strike force, composed of crack troops, mainly cavalry, recruited from armies on the Danube, in Asia and Africa. He minted a new gold coinage, the *multipla*, to pay this force. This special army seems not to have had a separate base and was probably stationed in cities, themselves now increasingly fortified. An extensive programme of qualitatively different fortifications had already begun, with huge towers and much thicker walls, all intended to endure long sieges. It was to continue throughout the following decades.

Gallienus' chief innovation seems to have been a policy of elastic defence. Replacing the earlier preclusive policy, this essentially meant giving up trying to hold the frontier at every point but instead waiting until the invading enemy could be advantageously attacked with superior forces. The policy bore fruit when Gallienus cornered an army of Goths at Nis in AD268. Unfortunately, although he had tried to secure the throne by forbidding senators from holding command, Gallienus failed to prevent the real threat from his own officers. Aureolus, his cavalry commander, declared himself emperor in AD268 and Gallienus abandoned his Gothic campaign to hurry back. In the subsequent siege of Milan, he was assassinated.

THE ILLYRIAN EMPERORS

Gallienus had come from the Roman nobility, but from now on a new breed of soldier-emperor was to dominate the succession: the Illyrian or Balkan emperors. First of these was Claudius II

"Gothicus", so-called because he defeated the Goths in AD269. His death from plague the next year led to the succession of Aurelian. Aurelian was indisputably a great soldier: he repelled the Vandals, Marcomanni and Juthungi, crushed the Palmyrene revolt and reconquered Gaul, although he had to abandon Dacia. But he had other attributes: he showed unusual clemency to rebels such as Zenobia, queen of Palmyra, and Tetricus, the emperor of Gaul; he built the walls around Rome, which, still standing, perpetuate his name; he was severe towards extortionate officials, one of the banes of every administration, and he built a huge Temple of the Sun in Rome. His death – he was murdered by his private secretary for reasons that are unclear – was much mourned. A series of short-lived Illyrian emperors followed; all were murdered by their troops. Only one, Probus, reigned long enough, from AD276 to 282, to have much impact, again defeating various German invaders before being murdered. Two years after his death, Diocletian found himself emperor and inaugurated what would become a very different regime.

Above: The walls hastily constructed by the emperor Aurelian around Rome in the AD270s were the first walls Rome had needed for 300 years, and they have survived for 1,700 years.

Below: Greatest of the Illyrian emperors was Diocletian who reformed the empire.

THE TETRARCHS' ACHIEVEMENTS: AD284–305

The empire that the Illyrian-born soldier Diocletian gained in AD284 was less immediately imperilled than it had been 20 years earlier, but it was still in a highly precarious state. The military had been expanded but new ways of paying for it had not been found. Inflation continued, with the result that the armies were still being paid – when paid at all – either in kind, by exactions, or in almost worthless coinage. The cost of both bore crushingly on the taxpayers, who were faced with huge, unpredictable demands.

Above all, the problem of the succession, the cause of incessant, empire-wrecking civil war, remained unsolved. Only one emperor had died a natural death in the preceding 70 years. All the rest had been murdered, often by their own armies. Diocletian, however, managed to retire and die in bed, and two subsequent emperors (Constantius Chlorus and Galerius) also died a natural death. Diocletian might have assumed this was due to the Tetrarchy, that system

he had devised with four rulers – two senior Augusti and two junior Caesars, the latter the Augusti's designated heirs. In fact, it was almost entirely due to Diocletian's own *auctoritas*, the respect in which he was held, that led the other emperors to ask him to reassume the throne at their last meeting in November AD308, three years after his retirement. The almost farcical chaos that overtook the rigid tetrarchical system – with numerous emperors emerging or re-emerging – exposed its shortcomings. Chief among these was its total disregard for hereditary sentiment. As Constantine demonstrated when acclaimed by his father's army on the latter's death in York in AD306, this remained very powerful.

In another sphere, the Tetrarchy proved more successful. Diocletian saw that the empire needed more than one *imperator*, or supreme commander. In the almost constant wars, often fought on several fronts, the long absence of the emperor on one front could too easily provoke discontent, even rebellion, on another. This was probably why he made another Illyrian soldier, Maximian, a fellow Augustus – a policy pioneered by Marcus Aurelius – and then appointed junior Caesars. Diocletian also developed the policy (which had originated with Domitian 200 years earlier) of making the emperor appear truly imperial, even divine. This led to elaborate court ceremonies and palace hierarchies. Although a further strain on the taxpayer, these should not be over-stated. Compared to the army, the tetrarchical bureaucracy was still quite small.

Diocletian had mixed success with his financial and economic reforms. He issued his famous Edict of Maximum Prices in AD301, fixing maximum prices for a wide range of goods and services to counter inflation. The attempt failed.

Below: The north wall of Diocletian's Palace at Spalato (Split), Croatia, showing the ornate but massively built Porta Aurea (Golden Gate) built c.AD300. Diocletian's palace-fortress epitomized the spirit of the age, grandiose and yet defensive.

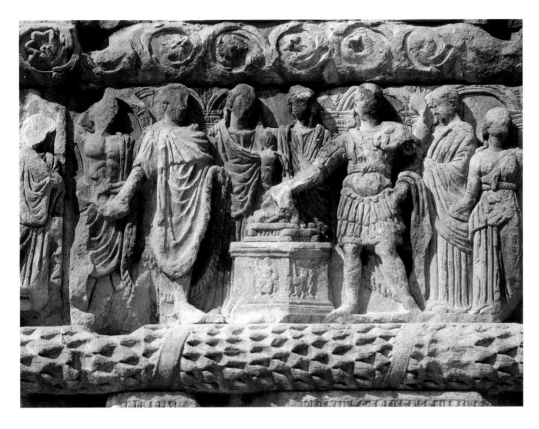

Left: Galerius (Augustus AD305–11) sacrificing to the pagan gods. Galerius instigated the last and worst persecution of the Christians in AD303–11. He thought them both sacrilegious and unpatriotic, but he failed to exterminate Christianity.

However, he had more success with taxation. He based taxes on a hypothetical unit that varied according to the quality of land held. Taxes were now assessed annually by the Praetorian prefect of each province. The *decurions* (officials) of the cities were made responsible for collecting taxes in their province. These were in kind and overwhelmingly agricultural. To ensure that tenant farmers paid them, they were increasingly tied to their land by imperial edicts; other trades were also declared hereditarily binding. Although oppressive, this system was superior to the naked exactions and chaos of the previous century.

MILITARY SUCCESSES

In one sphere, the Tetrarchy was undoubtedly successful: the military. The army was again expanded – to perhaps 500,000 men – with a formal separation of the frontier troops, the *limitanei*, commanded by a *dux* (leader), from the *comitatenses*, the mobile forces under the commands of *comites*, counts, not tied to specific frontiers. These battle troops were no longer under the control of the local governors, whose provinces were much reduced in size if they were increased in number, for a dual system of civilian and military government had by now been established. The aim, successful but superfluous as it turned out, was to prevent provincial governors from revolting.

But army commanders continued to rebel. With these armies, often stationed in camps so heavily fortified that they begin to deserve the name of castles, Diocletian and his colleagues won a series of major campaigns, most notably that of Galerius against the Persians in AD297–8, which gained a new province. At the same time, Constantius was regaining Britain from a usurper. His victory was more typical of the generally defensive victories of a defensive age. It epitomizes the real but limited achievements of the Tetrarchy, principally the sharing of power between several emperors, which led Gibbon to call Diocletian the second founder of the Roman empire. They allowed the empire to continue, in a controlled, rigid but viable manner, for further generations.

Below: This column shows Diocletian embracing his colleague Maximian.

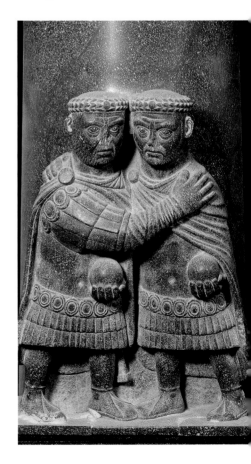

CONSTANTINE
THE LAST GREAT EMPEROR?

Above: One of the new solidi, *gold coins issued by Constantine, showing him in idealized perpetual youth – he was noted for his vanity, in his later years wearing a wig. His new coinage proved enduringly successful, however.*

Below: A relief from the Arch of Constantine in Rome illustrating his victory at the Battle of the Milvian Bridge in AD312 over his rival Maxentius. He attributed his victory later to a religious dream, but Maxentius was already an unpopular ruler.

The giant head and hands, sole surviving fragments of the titanic figure of Constantine that once dominated the Basilica Nova in Rome, seem to proclaim him one of the greatest emperors. His massive building programmes – at Trier, Rome and especially at Constantinople – reinforce this claim. Certainly, he changed the empire. He left it on the way to becoming Christian; gave it a new capital that became the centre of a new civilization (although he cannot have foreseen this); reformed the army again, if in ways that even contemporaries criticized; and defeated all his enemies, mainly Roman but also foreign – Franks, Sarmatians and Goths – before dying in bed, leaving the empire to his sons. How far he was a truly great ruler remains debatable.

Son of Constantius Chlorus, the Augustus of the west approved by Diocletian, Constantine was acclaimed by his troops at York in AD306. His rise to sole lordship of the empire was by typical rather than glorious means. His attack on Maxentius, ruler of Italy, in AD312 was standard action for an emperor controlling only the western provinces. His subsequent unprovoked attacks on his co-Augustus in the east, Licinius, had little justification except that of final success in AD324. If Constantine was more openly Christian than Licinius, the latter did not persecute Christians as a sect.

Constantine fought effectively against invading barbarians, from the Franks on the Rhine to the Goths on the Danube in his later years. These, along with success in more frequent civil wars, demonstrate military competence. But his military reforms – employing Germans in his crack *palatini* regiments, keeping large forces around him almost as a bodyguard – struck some contemporaries as more concerned to safeguard his power than his people. Quartering troops in towns also caused problems with military discipline. His military record was therefore mixed.

In founding Constantinople as his new capital – intending it less as a replacement for Rome than as a complementary eastern capital – Constantine showed great foresight. The best-defended site in Europe, at the crossroads of several major trade and military routes, Constantinople prospered, the one city in the empire that grew throughout the 4th century AD. According to legend, Constantine traced out its walls guided by a vision. In fact, his wall needed replacing by the Theodosian walls within a century, as the city's population approached three-quarters of a million people.

Constantine enduringly, if unwittingly, reformed the currency. This had been debased many times, so he issued a new coinage, the gold *solidus*, literally solid gold. It became widely accepted for many centuries after his death, a sign of Byzantine economic strength. This high-quality coinage was made possible by his pillaging of pagan temples. Treasures that generations had donated to their gods over the centuries were seized and often

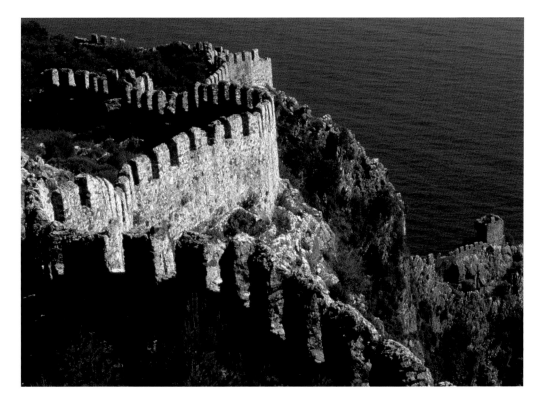

Left: Constantine built his new city of Constantinople (formerly Byzantium, today Istanbul) at a strategic position overlooking the Bosphorus. He would deserve to be remembered as a ruler touched by greatness simply for choosing this superb site for his new capital.

melted down. This was despoilation on a scale comparable with Henry VIII's dissolution of England's monasteries in the 1530s. But the *solidus* was a high-value coin, no good in daily use where inflation continued. Constantine's tax reforms were mixed; his taxes were so onerous that fathers reputedly sold their daughters into prostitution to pay them.

THE FIRST CHRISTIAN EMPEROR?

Constantine's greatest fame is as the first Christian emperor. Certainly, he forged the linkage of empire and Church – in the east until 1453, in the west until the 11th century Investiture Conflict – and ensured that the empire ultimately became Christian. This took time, however. Mass conversions of peasants in Asia Minor were still being carried out 200 years later. Constantine's own religious beliefs remain uncertain. Like his father, he initially worshipped *Sol Invictus*, the Unconquered Sun. After victory at the Milvian Bridge in AD312, he began sporting Christian as well as pagan insignia on his standards, but the Edict of Milan in AD313 granted toleration to *all* faiths, not just

Christianity. Constantine seems to have developed an interest in theological speculation – it was the golden age for it – chatting in bad Greek to bishops at the Council of Nicaea in AD325, although he was thought not to understand abstruse doctrinal points. He favoured the Church by financial measures but did not discriminate against non-Christians – more than 90 per cent of the population – in the army or administration. He continued to use the pagan title *pontifex maximus* (chief priest), did not object to the renovation of temples in old Byzantium and was baptized only on his deathbed. Admittedly this was common at the time, baptism being thought to wash away all existing sins.

Constantine was the last emperor to rule the whole Roman world for a lengthy time (AD324–37). There would be other valiant emperors after him, but none who could be considered great. The empire that he left his successors still looked brilliant, powerful and wealthy. But the extravagances of his court and capital and the rapacity of his tax-collectors, along with his reliance on Germans, augured ill for its longer-term health.

Above: This aqueduct supplying Constantinople with water was begun by Constantine but completed in AD378 by the emperor Valens, whose name it bears. The city had from the start excellent water supplies, as well as huge cisterns to enable it to withstand long sieges.

CONSTANTINE'S HEIRS

It would be fair to say that Constantine's heirs had most of his vices and few of his virtues. The one exception, Julian, ended his reign in military disaster. On Constantine's death in AD337, the army mutinied and murdered many of his family. Constantine II, Constans I and Constantius II, the three surviving sons, divided the empire between them. Constantine was killed in AD340 attacking Constans, who became sole ruler of the European provinces, before being murdered in AD350. Constantius II refused to accept Magnentius, the new western ruler, and finally defeated him in AD353. The empire was now reunited, if exhausted by renewed civil strife.

Constantius was judged stupid and vain by contemporaries. He was certainly fond of showy display: on his triumphant entry into Rome in AD354, he posed immobile in his chariot as though made of ivory and gold. A fanatical Christian, he enforced Arianism (a belief later declared heretical) upon the empire and surrounded himself with sycophantic eunuchs. But he still needed a co-emperor and first chose his half-cousin Gallus in AD354. However, Gallus' highly erratic behaviour, which recalled Caligula's, led to his downfall. Constantius then turned to the sole surviving member of his family, Julian, the son of Constantine's half-brother Julius Constantius, one of the victims of the murders of AD337.

JULIAN

Until then, Julian had led the life of a philosophy student. Unwillingly called from Athens to become Caesar in Gaul in AD355, he astonished everybody by displaying military genius. Julian made

Above: Julian, sole emperor AD361–3, was the last pagan emperor. He was also almost the only later emperor to realize how high taxation was crushing the poorer people in the empire. His tax reforms, like his pagan restoration, however, proved short-lived.

Right: In AD363, Julian's army reached the walls of the Persian capital Ctesiphon, behind which stood its royal palace with its huge arch, but he failed to take it. In the subsequent retreat, Julian lost his life and Rome many of its best troops and half of upper Mesopotamia.

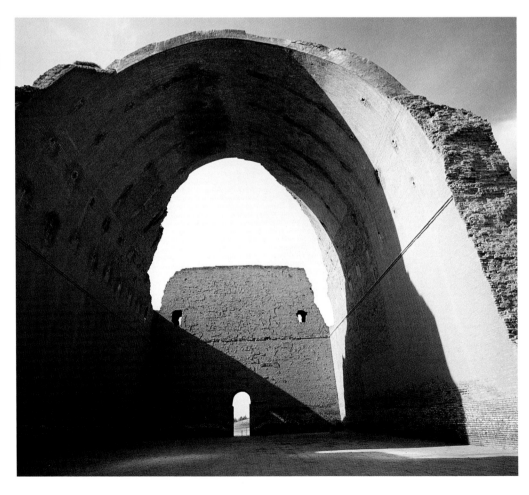

the small city of Paris (Lutetia) his base and recreated a proper army, repelling the barbarians. His greatest victory was at Strasbourg (Argentoratum) in AD357. Against an army of 35,000 Germans, he fielded some 13,000 men. After a long and hard-fought battle, the Romans won, with only 243 losses. Julian then crossed the river Rhine to campaign in Germany and re-established most of the Rhine frontier. He also tried to make the tax-collection system more efficient by stamping out corruption. He sacked some particularly extortionate officials, which boosted his popularity with the populace.

Constantius, now paranoid about his cousin's successes, ordered him to dispatch most of his best troops east in AD360. However, they revolted and acclaimed Julian Augustus: the empire seemed destined for yet another round of civil wars. Constantius turned his armies in the east to the west, but Julian struck first. The city of Aquileia in northeast Italy held out against his troops, but he marched east along the Danube and had reached Sirmium in the Balkans when news came of Constantius' death in late AD361. The empire was united again.

Julian's sole reign lasted only 18 months, but he filled it with activity. He sacked many of the well-paid imperial courtiers and officials. He then revealed his long-standing pagan beliefs, reopening pagan temples while banning Christians from teaching Greek and Roman classics – a major cultural blow. He even tried to encourage the Jews to rebuild the Temple in Jerusalem, as this would confound Christian prophecy. His gaze, however, was focused on the east.

PERSIAN NEMESIS

Julian decided to invade Persia for the usual Roman reasons: popular opinion expected the emperor to emulate Alexander the Great, and Persia appeared an enemy that could finally and profitably be defeated, unlike the drifting swarms of barbarians. An element of official revenge undoubtedly also played its part.

"We must destroy a dangerous nation whose swords are still wet with our brothers' blood!" Julian proclaimed, according to Ammianus. He gathered an army of 65,000 men, supplied by 1,000 boats and 100 galleys. He then sailed and marched down the Euphrates. Although he captured forts and defeated part of the Persian army, the main Persian forces avoided battle, instead adopting a scorched-earth policy to deny the Romans supplies. Julian decided to strike north-east across the Tigris into fresh lands, perhaps aiming to meet reinforcements from Mesopotamia, and the army began its retreat harassed by Persian mounted archers. Hurrying to help part of the army under attack, he left off his armour and received a fatal arrow wound, dying that night. Julian was the last significant non-Christian emperor, the last emperor with a real interest in Graeco-Roman culture, a writer of note and the only later Roman emperor to begin to comprehend the problems of the crushing weight of taxation upon the ordinary taxpayer. His death was a loss in more ways than might be expected.

Above: A coin of Constantine II, the oldest surviving son of Constantine I, whose reign of three years ended in AD340 when he was killed attacking his co-emperor and brother, Constans.

BRITAIN REGAINED AND ABANDONED

Above: The Romans continued to maintain and even expand their chain of fortresses and watchtowers, often on a large scale, all around the coasts of Britain until the very end of Roman rule in c.AD400. This suggests that they valued the province highly.

A realist in military matters, the emperor Septimius Severus nevertheless thought it was worth making the long journey north to Britain and campaigning for two years into Scotland. Britain mattered to Rome. The traditional view that the province required a military garrison disproportionate to its tiny population and wealth has been modified in recent years by archaeological finds. These suggest a far larger population than once thought – perhaps around four million. London, a great trading centre, was certainly the second biggest and richest city north of the Alps, with a population of around 40–50,000 at its 2nd-century AD peak. Whatever the exact figures, defending the island was clearly not just a matter of military prestige but also one of retaining a valuable province.

In the mid-3rd century AD, Britain was almost untouched by the waves of invasion that ravaged much of the empire, becoming part of Postumus' Gallic empire. Some Gallo-Romans may have migrated at this time to the relative security Britain offered, bringing their skills and wealth with them. Around this time, Saxon raiders along the shores of the Channel demanded the expansion of the existing *classis britannica*, the British fleet, and the construction of a chain of typically huge forts along the south-east coast. This fleet and the coastal forts formed the basis of the rebellion by the admiral Carausius and his successor Allectus in AD286–96, which for a moment made Britain a separate empire. But Allectus seems to have been an unpopular tyrant and by AD296 the Caesar Constantius Chlorus was poised to regain the province. His invasion met with little opposition; the citizens of London were particularly pleased that his troops reached the city before Allectus' unpaid Frankish mercenaries, who wanted to sack it. On his coins Constantius was hailed as the "restorer of eternal light".

Right: Foundations of a Roman watchtower survive high on the cliffs above Scarborough, Yorkshire, and formed part of the chain of forts and signalling stations constructed along the Saxon Shore of eastern Britain during the 3rd and 4th centuries AD.

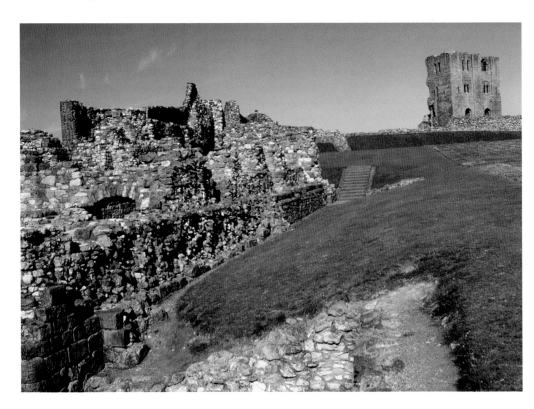

Constantius' time in Britain seems to have been fruitful. He recruited British *artifices* (skilled men) to restore the fortifications of Autun, one of Gaul's chief cities. He himself went north, again restored Hadrian's Wall, campaigned far into Scotland and finally died at York in AD306, a city whose walls were much strengthened during his reign.

The 50 years following Constantius' death have been called the golden age of villa life in Roman Britain. Again, recent archaeological evidence suggests that the villas built then were not the provincial half-timbered structures once thought. Some were large, complex and luxurious country houses, almost comparable in scale with those of 18th-century country houses, such as North Leigh in Oxfordshire. Cities now had their defences strengthened, but villas seem to have been unprotected, presumably because they were mostly in the safer, southern half of the province. This British wealth clearly persisted into the AD350s, despite the problems of Magnentius' unsuccessful bid for power, for the emperor Julian sent to Britain for 600 shiploads of wheat to feed his army on the Rhine in AD359.

THE FINAL COLLAPSE

Around AD367 all the barbarians around Roman Britain reputedly conspired to attack it in the same year: Caledonians from the north, Irish raiders from the west and Saxons from the east. Many Roman troops seem to have abandoned their posts, some even joining the barbarian looters who ravaged the whole island. The emperor Valentinian sent Count Theodosius, father of the future emperor, to Britain with some crack troops in AD368. Reaching London, Theodosius was greeted ecstatically by its citizens. From there, he issued proclamations offering amnesties to all troops who had deserted. Reforming the Roman armies in Britain, he systematically cleared the province, rebuilt the walls of many cities and

Left: The Notitia Dignitatum *listed in great detail Roman troop positions and fortresses in Britain and across the whole empire in AD395. This illustration actually dates from 1436 and so shows fortresses in Britain more imaginatively than literally.*

increased the number of coastal watch towers in the north and in Wales. Traditionally, he even marched north into Scotland again, naming the area between the two walls Valentia after the emperor.

However, Theodosius' restoration was Rome's last really effective intervention in Britain. Troops were withdrawn to support usurpers such as Maximus Magnus, who took many soldiers with him in his bid for the throne in AD383. Only 20 years later, many of the remaining troops were withdrawn by Stilicho, the west's effective ruler, and the remainder probably followed the usurper Constantine when he crossed to Gaul in AD407. Left to themselves, the British may have organized some defence, but by the AD430s the province had slipped out of the decaying Roman empire. In AD446 the Romanized Britons allegedly made a last appeal for help to Aetius, the west's great general, but in vain. He was too preoccupied with the Huns. The Saxons may have started settling in large groups along the east coast soon after, while the western areas were ruled by Romano-Celtic princes. This marked Rome's final abandonment of Britain.

Above: The remains of the Roman villa at Chedworth near Cirencester. Romano-British villas flourished up to the mid-4th century AD, often becoming large, even luxurious complexes of buildings, complete with baths and hypocaust central heating.

THE GOTHIC PROBLEM

Above: An aureus *(gold coin) showing the emperor Valens (AD364–75) who led the army of the east to disastrous defeat by the Goths at Adrianople in 378AD. He was an Arian Christian and persecuted orthodox Christians, pagans and Jews.*

By *c.*AD350, the Ostrogoths had established a huge realm from the Vistula to the Don, centred on the grasslands of the Ukraine well suited to their cavalry. Although not averse to raiding the Roman empire, here they posed little threat. Their Visigothic cousins meanwhile occupied the Dacian region. Both had converted to Christianity. The type that they learnt through a missionary, Ulfilas, was Arianism, which denied the divinity of Christ. However, it was not religion that led to the Goths' next clash with Rome.

Moving west across the steppes of Eurasia, the Huns burst into the world of Germans and Romans around AD373. The Ostrogoths, routed by them, fled west, driving their Visigothic cousins before them. "News spread through the Gothic peoples of a race of men, never before known, risen as if from under the earth and destroying all in their path," recorded Ammianus. The Visigoths,

panicking at tales of Hunnish ferocity, approached the Danube frontier and requested *receptio*, official permission to settle inside the empire. This had been granted to many Germans, often with success. The emperor Valens, senior emperor at the time, agreed provided the Goths surrendered their arms. He hoped that they would supply recruits for the army and farm deserted lands in Thrace. Ammianus described Valens as "overjoyed at the prospect". His joy was short-lived.

The Visigoths began crossing the Danube in late AD376. The river was swollen with rain and many drowned. The survivors were abused by corrupt Roman officials, who sold them dead dogs as food at inflated prices and raped their women. To pay for food, many Visigoths had to sell their children into slavery; the going rate was reputedly one dead dog per child. Meanwhile, Ostrogoths had also crossed the river. Fighting broke out and the Goths turned to pillaging the

Right: The battle of Adrianople in AD378 was a disaster from which the Roman empire never fully recovered, for it let the Goths into the empire en masse. *The army of the emperor Valens, hurrying from Constantinople, blundered upon the Gothic forces led by Fritigern, who had formed a defensive circular* laager *with their wagons in its centre. The battle was decided by the return of the foraging Gothic cavalry who encircled the Romans. Valens himself died in the battle.*

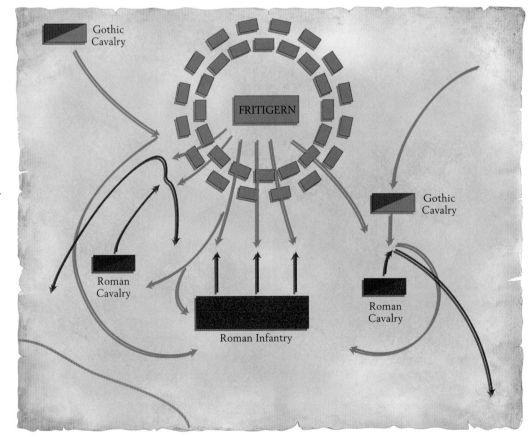

Gothic Cavalry

FRITIGERN

Gothic Cavalry

Roman Cavalry

Roman Cavalry

Roman Infantry

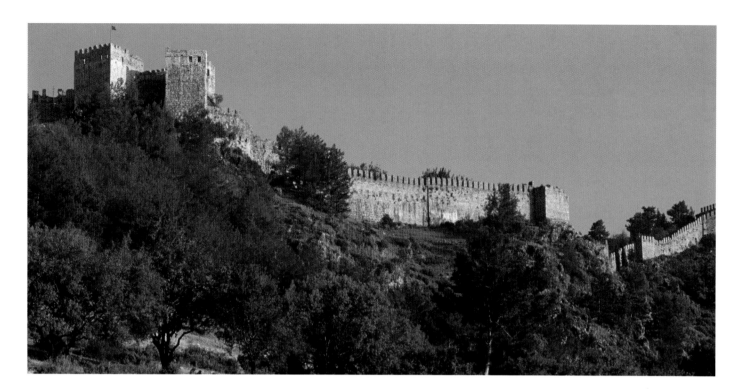

lands. They attempted to take Adrianople but its walls, as usual, defied them. The emperor Valens, deciding to deal with the invasion in person, assembled his armies at Constantinople in summer AD378 and rode north to meet the Goths.

THE BATTLE OF ADRIANOPLE

On a scorching hot day in August AD378 the army of the east, with 60,000 men, approached Adrianople. The Romans, who had been marching all day, were tired and thirsty, but when they saw the Goths ahead, Valens decided to attack at once. He was misled by reports that there were only 10,000 armed Goths ahead and wanted the glory of victory before his co-emperor Gratian joined him.

The Visigoths had formed their wagons into a *laager* (circle). Fritigern, the Visigothic leader, sent out for his cavalry, which was foraging, and for his Ostrogoth allies and their cavalry. Roman skirmishers seem to have begun the battle before Valens intended, for the Roman lines were not fully formed when the Visigoths counter-attacked, driving the skirmishers back into the Romans' main troops. The Gothic cavalry returned and, catching the Roman cavalry in the flank, drove it

from the field. Despite this, the Roman infantry in the centre rallied and, until sunset, the battle raged outside the *laager* like "the waves of the sea", according to Ammianus. However, the Gothic cavalry so tightened its grip on the encircled Romans that the soldiers could no longer wield their weapons effectively. Valens himself fell in the battle and his army fell with him.

Two-thirds of this great army was destroyed, but the Goths were unable to capitalize on their victory. They could not even capture Adrianople, with Valens' treasure and huge supplies within it, and their attack on Constantinople was a complete failure. Even so, two large Roman armies commanded by emperors had been defeated in 15 years. The new emperor Theodosius was forced into a wholesale policy of appeasement. He let the Visigoths settle *en masse* inside the empire in Pannonia and the Ostrogoths in Moesia. Further, he recruited Goths into the army, not just as individuals or small groups, but in whole tribes commanded by their chieftains. While earlier Germans had been Romanized by service in the imperial army, the Roman army now rapidly became barbarized.

Above: Nothing remains of the original walls around Constantinople (Istanbul) built by Constantine I in AD324. Later superseded by the Theodosian walls, they repulsed the Goths.

Below: Theodosius I (AD379–95), presents laurel crowns to the winners of a chariot race in Constantinople. The city shared Rome's urban amusements and also her imperial aspirations.

THE FATAL WINTER

Above: Theodosius I was the last emperor to rule the whole Roman empire.

Below: The interior of the Porta Nigra (Black Gate) at Trier.

In the later 4th century AD, the Rhine frontier looked relatively secure. It had been restored first by Julian and then by Valentinian (AD364–75), who had built or rebuilt many forts along it. He had even crossed the river once more to campaign in Germany, more than 400 years after Julius Caesar first crossed it. Valentinian was the last Roman general ever to do so.

Central to the defence of the frontier was the great fortified capital of Trier (Augusta Trevorum). Trier had replaced Lyons as the first city of Gaul in the 3rd century AD and was progressively fortified and adorned under the emperors Postumus, Constantius Chlorus and Constantine, whose capital it was for six years (AD306–12). A huge basilica, baths, palace and gates – the still-surviving Porta Nigra – and the large area enclosed by its massive walls testify to its

wealth. Set about three days' march back from the Rhine frontier in the fertile Moselle valley, the city of Trier had good communications with the Rhine front to the east and with the rest of Gaul behind it. From it, one road ran due west to Reims, another north-east to Coblenz on the Rhine, another south-west.

The lower Rhine below Cologne, where the river often overflowed its banks and so was hard to patrol, was abandoned as a frontier, probably early in the 4th century AD. However, a new *limes* stretched west from Cologne along the line Maastricht–Tongre–Bavay–Tournai–Boulogne. Roman outposts remained as far north as the Rhine's mouth, but this *limes* linked the Rhineland with the Channel and so with Britain. South along the Rhine's banks ran a line of much-strengthened frontier forts, manned with *limitanei*. However, all fortifications were useless without enough soldiers. In AD383 a rebel general in Britain, Magnus Maximus, was proclaimed emperor by his troops. He crossed to Gaul and held court at Trier from where he ruled the westernmost three provinces and was recognized (reluctantly) by Theodosius I. When Magnus marched south into Italy in AD388 to be defeated by Theodosius, he must have taken troops from Gaul and Britain – mobile *comitatenses* rather than stationary *limitanei*. Both were needed in the north.

By AD395, after another round of civil wars, the empire was divided between the sons of Theodosius: the ineffectual Arcadius in the east and the even more incompetent Honorius in the west. Stilicho, a Vandal by birth but deeply Romanized, was to govern the western empire until his murder in AD408, in some ways very effectively, but his attention was focused on the Danube and Italy, to the fatal neglect of the Rhine.

Around AD400, Germany was in turmoil. Suebians, Burgundians, Gepids and Vandals (cousins of the Goths) were

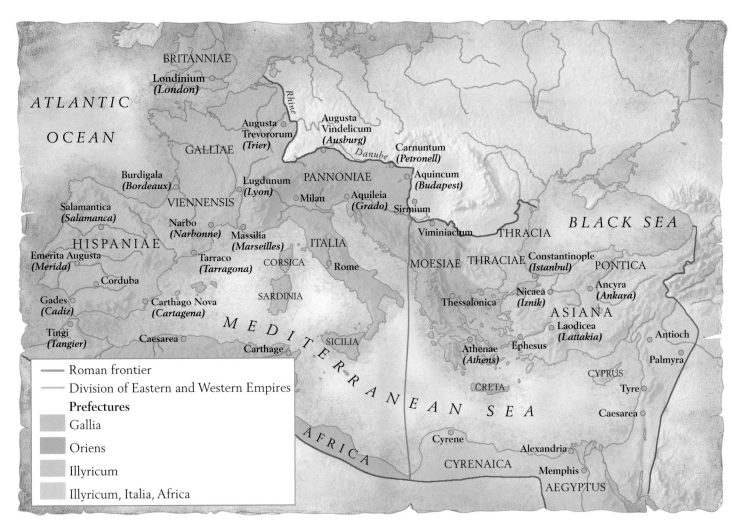

ATLANTIC OCEAN

BRITANNIAE
Londinium
(London)

GALLIAE

Augusta
Trevororum
(Trier)

Rhine

Augusta
Vindelicum
(Ausburg)

Danube

Carnuntum
(Petronell)

Burdigala
(Bordeaux)

Lugdunum
(Lyon)

PANNONIAE

Aquincum
(Budapest)

VIENNENSIS

Milan

Aquileia
(Grado)

Sirmium

BLACK SEA

Salamantica
(Salamanca)

Narbo
(Narbonne)

Massilia
(Marseilles)

ITALIA

Viminiacum

THRACIA

HISPANIAE

Tarraco
(Tarragona)

CORSICA

Rome

MOESIAE

THRACIAE

Constantinople
(Istanbul)

PONTICA

Emerita Augusta
(Merida)

Corduba

SARDINIA

Thessalonica

Nicaea
(Iznik)

ASIANA

Ancyra
(Ankara)

Gades
(Cadiz)

Carthago Nova
(Cartagena)

Laodicea
(Lattakia)

Antioch

Tingi
(Tangier)

Caesarea

MEDITERRANEAN SEA

Carthage

SICILIA

Athenae
(Athens)

Ephesus

Palmyra

CYPRUS

Tyre

CRETA

Caesarea

AFRICA

Cyrene

CYRENAICA

Alexandria

Memphis

AEGYPTUS

—— Roman frontier
—— Division of Eastern and Western Empires
Prefectures
  Gallia
  Oriens
  Illyricum
  Illyricum, Italia, Africa

pressing on older-established groupings such as the Franks and Alamanni, all of them alarmed by the advance of the Huns to the east. The winter of AD406–7 was unusually severe and the Rhine froze all the way down to the sea. On the very last day of AD406, a horde, perhaps 300,000 strong, led by the Vandals crossed the river. Trier was sacked so thoroughly it never recovered. (The fact that its great walls could not repulse the barbarians suggests that the city was hardly defended.) Other garrisons cowered uselessly behind their walls, deprived of the *comitatenses* essential to strike back. The barbarians pushed on through the frozen countryside, the Vandals finally crossing the Pyrenees into an almost undefended Spain. With them went the Suebians and the Alans, an Iranian people. The Burgundians turned due south, settling at first around Lake Geneva before expanding to occupy the

land that still bears their name. The Alamanni took Alsace, annexing that area for the Germanic world. Meanwhile, further north, in a less rapid but more enduring conquest, the Franks were pushing slowly but irreversibly forward, first to the Somme, then to the Loire. By AD496 they had conquered most of Gaul, giving it a new name: France.

In AD416 the Visigoths, acting now as *foederati* for Rome, temporarily drove the invaders of Spain into the far north-west, but the Vandals were not defeated. By AD429 they had overrun southern Spain (whose name Andalucia recalls their stay) and soon after began their conquest of North Africa, Rome's vital granary. By AD439, they had captured its capital Carthage, the western empire's second city. They had completed a long and profitable journey from their crossing of the frozen Rhine. As a result, the western empire was now doomed.

Above: The Roman empire c.AD400.

Above: An ivory diptych (double panel) dated AD406 shows the consul Probus and Honorius, the disastrously ineffectual emperor of the west (AD395–423), in whose reign Rome was sacked by the Goths in AD410.

THE SACK OF ROME

Above: An ivory panel of Stilicho (c.AD365–408), the regent of the west for the child-emperor Honorius. Though a competent general, Stilicho's devious negotiations with the Goths finally led to his death and left Rome at their mercy.

Right: Alaric's Visigoths ride into Rome. In fact, Rome's capture and sack was less dramatic but still epochal.

The sack of Rome by the Visigoths in AD410, although a crucial moment in world history, was not as dramatic as many might expect. Pictures of wing-helmeted barbarians brandishing bloody axes over weeping maidens, while palaces, libraries and temples burn in the background, exaggerate. The actual sack, although damaging materially as well as psychologically, was, by the age's standards, restrained, partly because the Visigoths were Christians. In any case, Rome's fall was caused more by the imperial government's miscalculations and vacillations than by Gothic desire to ravage the city. What the Visigoths wanted – and finally got – were titles, land and money for serving as Rome's ultimately surprisingly faithful *foederati* in Gaul. The cause of the sack of Rome lies as much with incompetent Roman government as with rapacious invaders.

Stilicho, who became regent of the western empire for the child-emperor Honorius in AD395, seemed to spend as much time intriguing against his rivals in Constantinople, where he aspired to become regent, as in repelling invaders. However, he was good at the latter. On two occasions he had the Visigoths, led by Alaric, at his mercy after defeating them: in western Greece in AD395 and in northern Italy in AD402. Both times he let them escape, perhaps because his troops were incapable of pursuit or maybe for less honourable motives. Yet although he may have played the Goths off against the eastern government at times, he was no traitor; he was merely trying to use them as Theodosius I had done. This appeasement led to his death, when public opinion turned against him for the loss of Gaul to Vandal, Suebian and other invaders in AD408. His murder was followed by the slaughter of many German mercenaries in the Roman army and the exodus of 30,000 others to join Alaric, gravely weakening the field army.

After extracting titles and money from the eastern empire and pillaging the Balkans, Alaric decided that the west offered richer pickings. The news of the death of Stilicho, which left the empire without a protector, led to three further

Visigothic invasions of Italy, the first in October, AD408. Bypassing the fortified cities and moving south, the Goths reached Rome and marched on to the port of Ostia. The Aurelianic walls around Rome, which had recently been strengthened and repaired, presented formidable barriers that should have repelled almost any barbarian. However, Rome was a populous inland city: it could be starved into surrender.

The Visigoths themselves also faced starvation, for they had no supply train. The first siege ended inconclusively when Alaric accepted a huge bribe of 5,000lb (2,268kg) of gold, 30,000lb (13,600kg) of silver and 3,000lb (1,360kg) of pepper. The second siege ended when Alaric installed a puppet emperor, Attalus, in Rome, who made him Field Marshal of the West (*magister utriusque militum*). When Attalus failed to please Alaric, the latter marched for a third time on Rome. The Ravenna government may have been pursuing a policy of attrition, hoping that the Goths would starve faster than the citizens of Rome and so be forced to retreat. If so, the strategy failed lamentably. On the night of 24 August AD410, someone – a Roman concerned at the sufferings of starving citizens, a disaffected slave – opened the Salarian Gate and the Goths entered the Eternal City. The unthinkable had happened.

THE AFTERMATH OF THE SACK

The Goths spent a mere three days in Rome, which had no food for their hungry army. Although they did not destroy the great city, they ransacked it and when they rode south they took with them Galla Placidia, the 16-year-old half-sister of the emperor Honorius. The shock of the sack meanwhile travelled round the Roman world. In Bethlehem, St Jerome was stunned, and in Africa St Augustine was moved to write his masterpiece, *The City of God*, to rebut pagan allegations that Rome's fall was due to its desertion of its ancestral deities in favour of Christianity.

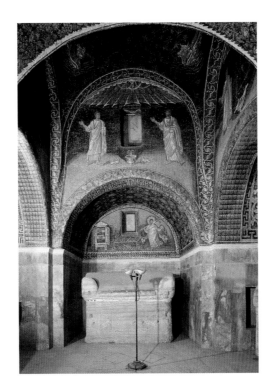

Left: The Mausoleum of Galla Placidia (lived AD388–450) at Ravenna. She was the sister of the emperor Honorius, mother of Valentinian II and effective empress of the west in her later years. Though strong-willed, her rule was nearly as disastrous as her brother's due to her personal vendetta with Aetius, Rome's last great general.

The Visigoths reached the Straits of Messina, as Alaric wanted to conquer Africa. However, storms dispersed his fleet and he himself died on the way back through Italy. (Legend says that he was buried under a river briefly diverted for the purpose.) His successor Ataulf led the Visigoths out of Italy into south-west Gaul, where he married Placidia, showering her with Roman booty. Constantius III, who now became co-emperor, refused to accept this situation. Using Rome's monopoly of naval forces, he drove the Goths into Spain, where Ataulf was killed. The next Visigothic king, Vallia, agreed to return Placidia to the Romans and become a *foederatus*, in exchange for receiving lands around Toulouse. In Spain, Vallia campaigned against barbarian invaders while Constantius, capturing the city of Arles, re-established partial Roman control over southern and central Gaul. By AD421, when Constantius died, the Roman empire in the west seemed to have survived the ultimate disaster. However, unnoticed by the court in Ravenna, the Vandals, escaping the Visigoths, had occupied Andalucia by AD422 and were casting their eyes on Africa.

Below: An early 5th-century AD ivory showing Serena, niece of the emperor Theodosius I, who married Stilicho. Although of Vandal ancestry, Stilicho was very much part of the Roman imperial establishment and not remotely "barbarous".

THE FALL OF ROME
HUNS, VANDALS AND AETIUS

Above: Alaric, king of the Huns (AD434–54), was Rome's most ferocious enemy, but he actually harmed the empire less than the cunning Vandal king Gaiseric, who seized Africa and sacked Rome itself in AD455.

As long as the western empire ruled the seas and could control Africa, the coasts of Spain, southern Gaul and Italy itself, it could hope to survive. However, the growing threat from the Huns, excessive preoccupation with Gaul at the expense of Africa and endless palace conspiracies combined to wreck the empire's last hopes of survival. When it finally collapsed, it did so almost unnoticed, having become irrelevant to most people.

The deaths of Constantius III in AD421 and Honorius two years later left Rome leaderless. Galla Placidia, Constantius' widow, managed, with east Roman help, to get her son Valentinian III on to the throne in Ravenna by AD425. Placidia was regent for her son at first. Unfortunately, she loathed Aetius, the Danubian-born soldier who now emerged as Rome's last effective general. Aetius had been a hostage of both the Visigoths and Huns. He got on well with the latter, understanding barbarians better than most Romans, but he was soon caught up in palace intrigues. Boniface, governor of Africa, first quarrelled with Placidia and then was reconciled, receiving the lofty title of *patricius*. Aetius, realizing that Placidia meant to destroy him, raised an army. With it, he fought Boniface in a great battle near Rimini. Although Boniface won, he died of his wounds and Aetius regained control of the government with Hunnish help by AD433. Meanwhile, Africa was being lost.

In AD429, Gaiseric, the Vandal king, led his 80,000 people across the Straits of Gibraltar into Africa. By AD431 he controlled the western African provinces. The recall of Boniface to Italy to fight Aetius allowed the Vandals to consolidate their conquests and they were accepted as *foederati* by Aetius. However, they soon resumed their attacks. By AD439, Gaiseric had captured Carthage, the second city in the western empire, giving him a fleet and control of the vital grain supply to Rome. The loss of Carthage was disastrous to the empire, but Ravenna agreed by a treaty of AD442 to accept the Vandals. Valentinian even promised to let his 5-year-old daughter marry Gaiseric's son, Huneric. Soon Gaiseric began extending his realm, capturing Sardinia, Corsica and Sicily, while his pirates raided as far as Greece. However, Aetius had his attention focused elsewhere.

In the AD430s Aetius had emerged as the clear arbiter of affairs in Gaul. In AD436 he called in the Huns to control the restless Burgundians – they killed 20,000 of them in battle – while his own troops drove the Visigoths back from Narbonne. In AD446, the despairing Britons even appealed to him for help, without success. By then, other even worse problems were emerging.

Below: This ivory shows Aetius, the last Roman general worthy of the name, presiding as consul over the games in Rome.

THE LAST VICTORY

In AD434 Attila became co-king of the Huns, whose empire stretched from Germany to the Volga. He soon killed his brother and terrorized the eastern empire into paying him tribute. In AD450 a new eastern emperor, Marcian (AD450–57), refused to pay any more. Attila turned for compensation to the weaker west where he had a strange excuse. Valentinian III's sister Honoria had had an affair with her steward. When this was discovered, she was kept in seclusion but smuggled a ring to Attila, asking for help. Seizing this excuse, and demanding half the empire as his dowry, Attila invaded Gaul. Only Paris resisted his 300,000 strong hordes and Attila sacked city after city with horrifying brutality. The Visigoths joined Aetius and, at Châlons-sur-Marne, their combined forces met Attila. The battle raged all day and left *cadavera vero innumera* (truly numberless corpses). The Romans threatened the Hunnish flank, but it was the Visigoths who bore the brunt and Theodoric, their king, was killed, which makes him an unsung saviour of western civilization. At the day's end, Attila decided to retreat for the only time in his life.

Next year, Attila invaded Italy. Aetius had no troops this time, but Pope Leo I rode north and somehow persuaded Attila to withdraw. Within two years he was dead, his empire disintegrating with him. Aetius, the architect of his defeat, did not live to enjoy it, however, for Valentinian III, in a jealous rage at the general who had outshone him, personally killed him. Early in AD455, two of Aetius' former soldiers killed Valentinian in turn, and the empire began its final decline. Gaiseric now appeared with a huge fleet, taking a leisurely 14 days to sack Rome, removing even the gilded roof tiles from the temples.

Various emperors, mostly puppets of German generals, followed over the next 20 years. Only Marjorian (AD457–61) deserves the title. He made a brave, if unsuccessful, attempt to defeat Gaiseric, before being murdered by Ricimer, the German power behind the throne. Finally, in AD476, the boy emperor mockingly called Romulus Augustulus – in reference to Rome's first king and first emperor – was deposed by another German, Odovacer. The imperial insignia were sent to Constantinople, the fiction being that the empire had been reunited. Few people outside Italy noticed.

Above: The Battle of Châlons-sur-Marne in AD451, when Aetius repulsed the Huns and their allies under Attila, was the last Roman victory, albeit one gained with Visigothic aid and resulting in little more than a draw. But Gaul was saved from the Huns.

WHY ROME FELL AND BYZANTIUM SURVIVED

Above: Theodora was allegedly a prostitute before she married the emperor Justinian. She then became one of the greatest empresses, rallying her despairing husband during the "Nike" riots and helping him rule the resurgent empire.

Right: The Mediterranean world c.AD526 after the final fall of Rome. Of the many barbarian successor states, Theodoric's Ostrogothic kingdom in Italy seemed far the strongest and richest, but it was soon reconquered by the Byzantines (east Romans), who had never accepted the loss of the west. Only the Franks and the still pagan Saxons formed enduring kingdoms.

Edward Gibbon, author of *The Decline and Fall of the Roman Empire* (1776), summarized the causes of Rome's fall as the "triumph of barbarism and religion". Gibbon meant that, while barbarians threatened the empire from outside, Christianity undermined it from within, encouraging men to neglect their duties as soldiers to become monks or priests. But his explanation ignores the survival of the more Christianized east Roman (Byzantine) empire for 1,000 years.

Some moralists once saw in the fall of the Rome the "wages of sin" – meaning sexual excesses. Debauchery, according to this theory, so rotted the moral fibre of once upright Romans that they could hardly crawl from their marble baths. They perhaps read Gibbon's description of the teenaged emperor Gordian III whose "22 acknowledged concubines

and… 62,000 volumes attested the variety of his inclinations… it appears that both the one and the other were designed for use rather than ostentation". Gordian (reigned AD238–44) was an ineffectual emperor, but no historian today attributes his failure to his sex life or bibliophilia.

Most later Roman emperors were neither nerveless nor effete. The great soldier–emperors of the 3rd and 4th centuries AD, such as Aurelian, Constantine I or Valentinian I, were energetic, brave generals. Their military efforts were ultimately in vain, however. This has led historians to seek social and economic causes for Rome's fall.

A plausible culprit is malaria. This may have spread as deforestation of mountains led to the formation of more marshes ideal for malaria-bearing mosquitoes. Malaria reduced the overall population, undermining the health of survivors. Similarly, plague, which hit the empire from AD165 on, must have played a part. But recent studies show that climate change did not affect the empire.

Each theory may explain an aspect of Rome's decline but cannot account for the survival of the similarly afflicted eastern empire. This rode out the 5th-century AD cataclysm relatively unharmed, to enjoy a golden age in the 6th century AD. Some historians have given up trying to explain the fall of Rome. Others have minimized the importance of imperial collapse, stressing the continuity of life in western Europe after AD476. Certainly, the German invaders had little new to offer, often perpetuating Roman customs. In Italy under the Ostrogoths c.AD500, the Senate still sat in Rome, aqueducts flowed and races were still run in the circus. Meanwhile, the Catholic Church expanded across western Europe and Latin survived, if mutating into varied forms. The one exception was Britain, where Anglo-Saxons deleted Romano-British culture. The Belgian historian Henri Pirenne argued that the real break between ancient and medieval worlds came in the 7th century AD with the Arab conquest. This divided the Mediterranean world, turning North Africa, Syria and Egypt away from Europe and towards the Islamic east.

For many people the question of why Rome fell remains as intriguing as ever. It is possible to discern major causes. Some were social and economic, a few were psychological and religious (shown by the growth in monasticism). However, political and military factors played an enormous and ultimately fatal part.

THE RICH–POOR DIVIDE

Essentially, Rome's civilization was urban, "a confederacy of cities". Although most of the empire's cities had 10–30,000 inhabitants, and only a handful were much bigger, most cities (outside Egypt) were self-governing. This was partly

because many had old and proud civic traditions, but more because the Principate lacked the governmental machinery for direct rule. Instead, it relied on unpaid officials, the decurions.

These men formed a middle group or class beneath the aristocracy of senators and equestrians. They included former centurions, local officials and landowners. From the 3rd century AD, this group was burdened with onerous tax demands by central governments. Faced with rebellions if they tried to collect the taxes and personal ruin if they did not – for the government made them personally liable – some decurions abandoned urban life altogether and withdrew to the country. Urban life, once so vigorous, decayed.

The plight of the peasants was worse. Most land was cultivated by labourers working as tenants for large landowners. After AD200, facing increasingly heavy taxation, some peasants became outlaws – central Gaul was ruled by the Bagaudae robber league – but most sought the protection of landowners to defend them from rapacious officials. This hurt both imperial revenues and farming. By AD400, up to a third of agricultural land in Africa, the west's most productive region, had gone out of cultivation.

Above: Justinian I (AD527–65), here shown in mosaics at Ravenna flanked by his courtiers, was the greatest east Roman, or Byzantine, emperor. He reconquered half the western empire and ordered the final and permanent codification of Roman law.

Below: The Cathedral of Hagia Sophia (Holy Wisdom) was Justinian's supreme monument in Constantinople (Istanbul), marking a radical development in late Roman architecture. Later a mosque, it is today a museum.

Above: Constantine I (AD306-37) was the effective if unwitting founder of the Byzantine empire by choosing Byzantium, so superbly sited, as his new capital, and also by converting to Christianity.

MILITARIZATION, BARBARIZATION

Under the Republic, civilians had usually controlled the military. Citizens were expected to fight for the city but were forbidden to bear arms within the city's sacred *pomerium* (boundary). Augustus upheld this tradition. In Rome he was merely *princeps*, first citizen. The Praetorian guard, although really part of the regular army, was always seen as different. This noble fiction, fraying as early as Domitian, survived until the reign of Septimius Severus (AD193–211). Under the Severans, who posted a legion near Rome, the reality of military power became brutally apparent.

After Gallienus (AD253–68) banned senators from army commands, most civilians lost all experience of – and taste for – military life. The military became a caste apart, recruited no longer from the cities but from less Romanized border peoples such as the Illyrians. Increasingly, these were supplemented by non-Roman auxiliaries. Earlier emperors had employed auxiliaries, but these had been under Roman command. From the time of Constantine, however, Germans came to dominate the best regiments, the *Palatini*. After the disaster at Adrianople in AD378, whole peoples of dubious loyalty, like the Visigoths, were enrolled in the Roman armies. If barbarians never accepted Rome's draconian discipline, soon Roman troops also rejected it. Vegetius, writing c.AD400, lamented the decline of the old discipline, which had once made the Roman soldier so effective. Even worse, Roman armies too often fought each other.

CIVIL WARS WITHOUT END

"The Roman world is collapsing… Fighting among ourselves costs us more than fighting our enemies." The lament of St Jerome from Bethlehem in Palestine comes from AD396, just as the western empire began to collapse. Jerome was primarily worried about the Huns then threatening the eastern provinces, but his diagnosis was accurate. Even when the empire was being overrun, pretenders still denuded frontiers of their garrisons.

A crucial weakness of the Roman empire was its lack of an accepted system of succession. Monarchies are normally hereditary. In theory, the empire was not a monarchy, but emperors exploited dynastic feeling where they could, even if they had catastrophic heirs. Diocletian devised an elaborate succession for the Tetrarchy. Unfortunately, he ignored hereditary sentiment among the army and imperial contestants themselves, so that his system, too, failed. Armies continued to proclaim emperors to the end. In AD407, troops in Britain followed the pretender Constantine to Gaul, thereby stripping Britain of its last troops.

The main imperial government behaved no better. The two most capable west Roman generals of the 5th century, Stilicho and Aetius, both fell victim to palace coups. Personal feuds between generals, encouraged by the empress Galla Placidia, led to the loss of Africa to the Vandals. Such court conspiracies were far worse in the west than the east.

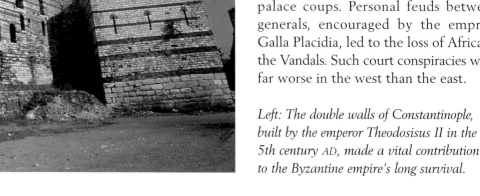

Left: The double walls of Constantinople, built by the emperor Theodosisus II in the 5th century AD, made a vital contribution to the Byzantine empire's long survival.

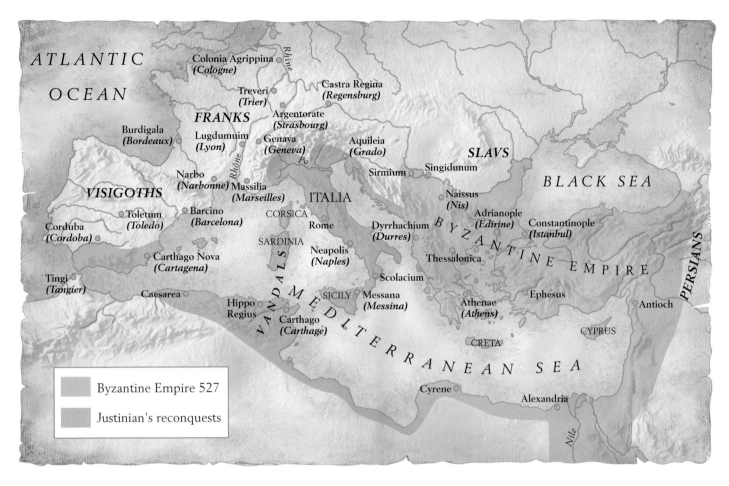

ATLANTIC OCEAN

Colonia Agrippina
(Cologne)

Rhine

Treveri
(Trier)

Castra Regina
(Regensburg)

FRANKS

Argentorate
(Strasbourg)

Burdigala
(Bordeaux)

Lugdumuim
(Lyon)

Genava
(Geneva)

Aquileia
(Grado)

SLAVS

Po

Rhone

Narbo
(Narbonne)

Massilia
(Marseilles)

ITALIA

Sirmium

Singidunum

BLACK SEA

VISIGOTHS

Toletum
(Toledo)

Barcino
(Barcelona)

CORSICA

Rome

Dyrrhachium
(Durres)

Naissus
(Nis)

Adrianople
(Edirine)

Constantinople
(Istanbul)

Corduba
(Cordoba)

SARDINIA

Neapolis
(Naples)

Thessalonica

B Y Z A N T I N E   E M P I R E

Tingi
(Tangier)

Carthago Nova
(Cartagena)

Caesarea

Scolacium

SICILY

Messana
(Messina)

Athenae
(Athens)

Ephesus

Antioch

PERSIANS

Hippo
Regius

V A N D A L S

Carthago
(Carthage)

M E D I T E R R A N E A N   S E A

CYPRUS

CRETA

Byzantine Empire 527

Justinian's reconquests

Cyrene

Alexandria

Nile

BYZANTIUM'S STRENGTHS

The most obvious strength of the eastern empire was Constantinople's superb site. Its brilliantly fortified peninsula, coupled with a control of the sea that the Byzantines retained for centuries, made it impregnable to direct attack until the advent of gunpowder. (It fell to the crusaders in 1204 only through treachery.) Any enemy coming from the Danube would find his way blocked by its double walls. Persian and Arab invaders could not reach the European provinces. Its double walls protected not only palaces, libraries and churches, but also warehouses and workshops, for Constantinople became a great manufacturing and trading city, unlike Rome. Its many inhabitants considered themselves Christian Romans – "*Romaoi*" in Greek, the language they soon came to speak exclusively.

The eastern empire was also far richer than the west. Cities such as Antioch, Alexandria and Smyrna remained great trading centres. With their deep-rooted

urban traditions, they survived to profit from the general economic recovery by AD500. The east was fortunate in that the Persian front was quiet at this time. Persia had problems of its own. This let eastern emperors concentrate on their short European frontiers. If Goths and Huns ravaged the Balkans in the 5th century, the rest of the eastern empire avoided direct attack.

In the early 6th century, the emperor Anastasius I (AD491–518), a financial genius, reorganized the army and left a full treasury. Under the rule of Justinian I (AD527–65) a splendid Byzantine culture emerged, embodied in the cathedral of Hagia Sophia (Holy Wisdom), with its radical new design and gold-crusted two-dimensional art. East Roman power reached westward, reconquering Africa and Italy. Byzantium retained outposts in southern Italy until 1071. By shielding Europe from Arab attack for so long, Byzantium helped the survival of western Christian civilization as well as its own.

Above: The Byzantine Empire in the 5th and 6th centuries AD, *showing Justinian's reconquest of the richer parts of the west.*

Below: St Irene Church in Constantinople (Istanbul).

INDEX